Credible Threat

Oxford Studies in Digital Politics
Series Editor: Andrew Chadwick, Professor of Political Communication in
the Centre for Research in Communication and Culture and the Department
of Social Sciences, Loughborough University

Credible Threat

ATTACKS AGAINST WOMEN ONLINE AND THE
FUTURE OF DEMOCRACY

SARAH SOBIERAJ

OXFORD
UNIVERSITY PRESS

OXFORD
UNIVERSITY PRESS

Oxford University Press is a department of the University of Oxford. It furthers
the University's objective of excellence in research, scholarship, and education
by publishing worldwide. Oxford is a registered trade mark of Oxford University
Press in the UK and certain other countries.

Published in the United States of America by Oxford University Press
198 Madison Avenue, New York, NY 10016, United States of America.

© Oxford University Press 2020

The illustration is by Ruth Tam (2020) and she has retained the rights to the piece

Library of Congress Cataloging-in-Publication Data
Names: Sobieraj, Sarah, author.
Title: Credible threat : attacks against women online and the future of
democracy / Sarah Sobieraj.
Description: New York, NY : Oxford University Press, [2020] |
Series: Oxford studies digital politics series |
Includes bibliographical references and index.
Identifiers: LCCN 2020012856 (print) |
LCCN 2020012857 (ebook) | ISBN 9780190089283 (hardback) |
ISBN 9780190089290 (paperback) |ISBN 9780190089313 (epub)
Subjects: LCSH: Internet and women. | Online hate speech. |
Misogyny. | Sexual harassment | Sex discrimination against women.
Classification: LCC HQ1178 .S64 2019 (print) |
LCC HQ1178 (ebook) | DDC 004.67/8082—dc23
LC record available at https://lccn.loc.gov/2020012856
LC ebook record available at https://lccn.loc.gov/2020012857

9 8 7 6 5 4 3 2 1

Paperback printed by LSC Communications, United States of America
Hardback printed by Bridgeport National Bindery, Inc., United States of America

For Jim, Quinn, and Graham

Contents

Acknowledgments

This project was born of many hands, most directly those of the women who shared their stories with me. Most, though not all, of these women found their experiences with digital harassment deeply disturbing, even traumatic. Their willingness to trust another stranger and revisit these difficult experiences is a testament to their generosity and strength. Listening to each of them—digesting their wit, intelligence, and resilience—has been profound. I hope they feel represented in these pages and that it will not be long before we begin to divine ways to stem the tide of identity-based attacks online. There are ways. We simply need willingness.

Over the course of this research, I spent time in several vibrant interdisciplinary spaces where I was challenged, energized, and inspired. Near the start of this project, I was invited to visit the Social Media Collective at Microsoft Research New England and Development. I'm grateful to Siva Vaidhyanathan for facilitating that introduction, and to Tarleton Gillespie, Nancy Baym, and Mary Gary for the early sounding board and, somewhat later, the wonderful temporary working environment. I may never recover from the office envy! Around the same time, Nathan Matias worked with Jigsaw and the MIT Media Lab to pull together 35 academic and nonacademic researchers, advocates, and platform representatives working on online harassment to help set an agenda around the key question: What research do we need to make sense of and address this problem? I'm fortunate to have been among these folks and hope that this book contributes something—however small—to these efforts.

The National Institute for Civil Discourse Research Network has provided a thought-provoking and supportive intellectual space over the last several years. A special thank you to Robin Stryker and Rob Boatright for wrangling us all into one room. Listening to the members of that group makes my brain sparkle. That sparkly listening is made all the more impactful by the talk-a-mile-a-minute conversations that happen at the margins of those convenings. Going forward, let's add happy hour, so no one debates politicians' right to block people on Twitter in the women's restroom again.

This research also benefited from the scholarly incubators built by the Social Science Research Council (SSRC). Thanks to Alondra Nelson, Mike Miller, Jason Rhody, Sam Spies, and Adrianna DiSilvestro for building and facilitating the Disinformation Research Mapping Initiative, and to the ideas shared by Yochai Benkler, Joan Donovan, Sarah Jackson, Dave Karpf, Siva Vaidhyanathan, and Claire Wardle at the inaugural meeting. The SSRC was also the magician behind the curtain for the Workshop on Race, Gender, and Toxicity Online, organized and chaired by Talia Stroud and Gina Masullo. During that workshop, I had the great fortune of hearing from pioneers in the field whose work I have long admired and from talented graduate students poised to make an impact. Thank you for creating these intellectual communities and for all the administrative work that goes into making them wonderful.

This research was supported by funding from the National Institute for Civil Discourse, the Jonathan M. Tisch College of Civic Life at Tufts University, and a Senior Semester Leave from the College of Arts and Sciences at Tufts University that came at exactly the right time. Many thanks to Rob Boatright, Pawan Dhingra, Peter Levine, Chris Swan, and the Faculty Research Awards Committee at Tufts for facilitating.

Earlier opportunities to write have been helpful in shaping my thinking. Segments of the Introduction appeared in an earlier form in *Information, Communication, and Society*, and part of Chapter 5 draws on an essay about Omar Ilhan that I wrote for the SSRC's MediaWell.

I owe thanks to many Jumbos. I'm thankful to Bárbara Brizeula and Jim Glaser for helping to make Tufts a place where I can enjoy teaching and find the time to focus on my research. I'm also grateful to my colleagues in and outside of sociology for their camaraderie and support. As a case in point, while writing this book I was also up for promotion; tenure and promotion cases make a lot of work for a lot of people. Thank you to Freeden Blume Ouer, Paul Joseph, Helen Marrow, Rosemary Taylor, John LiBassi, and Erin Sullivan for their efforts on my behalf; to Debbie Schildkraut and Jeff Berry for their mentorship; and to all the letter writers who took time out of their lives to read and evaluate my work. Finally, special thanks to the Tufts European Center for three glorious summers spent teaching in the Alps while basking in the scenery, the tartiflette, and the companionship of spectacular colleagues, particularly Gabriella Goldstein, Michael Ullman, Dennis Rasmussen (now at Syracuse, but I forgive him), Hugo Beauchemin, Kendra Field, and David Gute. These magical escapes gave me a chance to step away, clear my head, and slow down. What a gift!

Tufts also overflows with wonderful students, and three in particular helped bring this book to fruition. Sarah Matthews and Erica Nork were indispensable research assistants, though I'm as grateful for the energy and curiosity they brought into my office as I am for their work. Talking with them regularly about the project (and listening to them discuss it with each other) reminded and re-reminded me how much I care about this work and love sociology. Shaan Merchant and I worked together on an adjacent project, but his kindness, compassion, and humility contributed by offering a powerful counter-narrative to the cruelty and hate at the core of this research. I also owe thanks to a special alum, Ruth Tam, who made time in her life to design the cover of this book. I hope the contents do it justice.

Many colleagues outside of Tufts provided valuable feedback, guidance, insight, and community along this journey. Thanks to Deana Rohlinger who is not only a stunningly efficient and reliable collaborator, but a badass to boot. Thanks also to Danna Young for the distinctive excitement and energy she brings to intellectual exchange (and also for her friendship). At the start of this project (and for several years prior), Tina Fetner and Jessica Fields helped me find my way. Thanks to you both. I have also found myself energized and enlightened by conversations with Dana Fisher, Jenn Lena, Dave Karpf, Angie Hattery, Maggie Rex, Jessie Daniels, Tarleton Gillespie, Jennifer Earl, Gina Masullo, Philip Cohen, Mark Kingwell, Rachel Sherman, Talia Stroud, and Ron Jacobs. Many thanks to you all. A special thank you to Andy Chadwick for his feedback, Angela Chnapko at Oxford for her insight and support, and Letta Page, who jumped in during the last two weeks of writing with sanity-saving support and detailed feedback.

Without reminders that alongside the ugliness at the heart of this book, there is abundant empathy, beauty, and joy, I could never have completed it. One of my favorite such reminders has been the languorous evenings around the fire with Irene Farmer, Eric Conti, and the Johnson family. Jim and I are so fortunate to have you as neighbors. Thank you to Rebekah Miner for being one of my favorite people to listen to/talk with, Kate McCampbell for keeping me (nearly) sane, and Angie Boylan for all of her charisma and grace. I look forward to being able to spend more time with each of you. Thanks also to

Shannon Scully, Tracey Spruce, and Amy Whitehead for reminding me that this imperfect stew we're swimming in is, at the very least, entertaining. Thank you, finally, to my partners-for-life Kristen Wallingford and Heather Laube. There are no words.

My father, John McGuire, is a wonderful listener, and I needed that support more over the last year than I have in a long time. Thank you, Dad, for everything. Meanwhile, Laurie McGuire, my one-of-a-kind mother, has provided a constant reminder that there is joy to be had—especially on Broadway. No matter where we are, though, I can still beat her at Jotto. I love you, Mom. Thanks also to Brenda McGuire, Jeb and Nikki McGuire, Maddie and Matt Martelli, Mary Lou Sobieraj and the whole Sobieraj-Forth-Westfall clan, Teena and Tom Fitzroy and the Rex-Spallina crew, the Buffalo McGuires (past and present!), and *all* the Dudmans for the comfort food, cocktails, conversation, group texts, board games, and banter. This is the good stuff.

Finally, I need to thank my favorite cast of characters: Jim, Quinn, and Graham Sobieraj. They know the whole truth of this book, and it was not pretty. Toward the end I was a fixture at my desk. I wrote every day, all day, all evening, and on weekends for longer than I expected or am willing to admit. And yet, somehow, rather than get irritated that I wasn't available for cooking or fun (or even out of my pajamas), Quinn and Graham never complained. Not once. They applauded how long and hard I worked. They told me I was "amazing," commended my grit, and said I was a role model (of all things). Quinn picked up my slack around the house. Graham ran to get me iced tea over and over again—even once in the pitch black of winter before 6 AM. Their magnanimity surprised me—they are teenagers, after all—but it shouldn't have. They learned this ethic of teamwork and support from my husband, Jim. And while this way of being in the world is as natural to him as breathing, it was not easy. Like being in silhouette, my long days became his long days, even when I wished it could have been otherwise. Thank you, Jim, Quinn, and Graham for rising to the occasion and continuing to inspire me. I am happy to report that I'm back in the game.

Credible Threat

Introduction

Weaponized Identities

In February 2018, three days after the shooting at Marjorie Stoneman Douglas High School in Parkland, Florida, ended the lives of 17 students, survivor Emma Gonzalez gave an 11-minute speech on gun control at a rally in Ft. Lauderdale, Florida. Several students made speeches that day, but Gonzalez's teary, rage-filled demand for public accountability and her "We Call BS" refrain captured attention. The news media took notice, and across social media, clips of her speech racked up countless likes and shares. On CNN's YouTube channel alone, her comments were viewed over 3 million times. And a single tweet containing the footage was retweeted nearly 130,000 times. Emma Gonzalez went viral. Passionate about working toward change, Gonalez joined twitter (@emma4change), where she gained hundreds of thousands of followers in a matter of days, surpassing and eventually more than doubling the number of followers enjoyed by the National Rifle Association.

Social media were instrumental in Gonzalez's ability to connect with other gun control advocates and to organize and promote the March for Our Lives a few weeks later. Still, the visibility and access afforded by platforms such as YouTube and Twitter were not without their costs. In addition to tweets from inspired teens and celebrity admirers around the world, Gonzalez received significant digital pushback. The pushback included reasoned arguments about the Second Amendment and stories about guns being used in self-defense, but it also contained identity-based attacks drawing on then 18-year-old Gonzalez's perceived gender, race, and sexual orientation. Much of the internet seemed united in an attempt to demean her. Tweets directed at her included remarks such as these:

Credible Threat. Sarah Sobieraj, Oxford University Press (2020). © Oxford University Press.
DOI: 10.1093/oso/9780190089283.001.0001.

@emma4change hi you lying slut .. I'm 22 years old currently in England and I just bought an nra membership .. im not even American .. but I bought it to give them more power u cunt

Too bad Nicholas Cruz didn't kill Emma Gonzalez. Ugly dyke bitch.

Also I'm not saying it is solely racism, but I do want to cum on Emma Gonzalez shaved head

The pushback was often even uglier in spaces less regulated than Twitter. On Reddit, one post about her read:

I see Coconut Head as a challenge, more than anything. Here is a woman who, in every single aspect, is absolutely revolting - her exterior AND her personality - yet I can't help but wonder what would be like, to plunge balls-deep into her repeatedly. That's right. Balls-deep. With no protection. I won't lie, I'm extraordinarily-hard while typing this. I want to grab this... thing... and that's what Coconut Head is, let's not delude ourselves, a "thing"... by the hips and ram mercilessly in and out of her quivering, malformed cunt with the force of a gladiatorial chariot, while she makes stupid faces and contorts orgasmically, unable to control her bodily reactions even if she wanted to. I would erupt violently inside that corrupt and corrupting womb as though the entire fate of humanity depended on my seed penetrating the foul walls of one of her ovaries, the electrical fusion from this coupling creating the Antichrist, as our combined, guttural, Chewbacca-like roars shattered glass and walls alike around us, the house toppling down while we lay there in a filthy, disgusting mess. Yeah. I reckon Coconut Head does it for me.

This commentary should give us pause because of its hate and violence. It should give us pause because this culture of abuse is widespread (Amnesty International 2018; Farrell et al. 2019; Mantilla 2015; Levey 2018). It should give us pause because it threatens the lives and liberties of those it targets. And it should give us pause because it has deleterious consequences for the strength of our democracy. Far too often, the chilling effect of this invective is lost. Those targeted are told not to give oxygen or attention to the trolls, to brush off and dismiss death threats and rape fantasies. If they leave Twitter or quit blogging, we reason that they have decided to stay above the fray, to save their thoughts for more fruitful venues—not that they have been effectively silenced. This kind of digital abuse must be understood as a struggle to control political discourse that reflects and reinforces existing social inequalities. This often gets lost. At least it was lost on me.

In 2012 and 2013, the headlines about Anita Sarkeesian, Zerlina Maxwell, and Caroline Criado Perez caught my attention. Sarkeesian, the feminist cultural critic who would later become a central target in the Gamergate attacks, faced a wave of disturbing digital abuse in response to her web series on sexism in video games. Perhaps the best known example being the "Beat Up Anita Sarkeesian" game, which allowed players to "punch" her photo and watch as each strike bruised and bloodied her face. Shortly thereafter, political commentator Zerlina Maxwell was in the news. While a guest on FoxTV's Hannity, Maxwell argued that rape prevention efforts would be better served by teaching men not to rape than by arming women. The response was a torrent of racialized and gendered digital attacks. Next, there were headlines about feminist writer and activist Caroline Criado Perez who was bombarded with violent threats in the wake of her successful campaign to add a woman's face to those represented on bank notes in the United Kingdom. It's risky to be a feminist in public, I thought.

I wasn't wrong, but when sexist attacks against journalists Amy Wallace and Amy Harmon became public in early 2014, it became clear that something bigger was at play. Wallace and Harmon were attacked in response to stories they had written on vaccines and genetically modified foods, respectively, and still the attackers speculated about their sexual behavior and flung the c-word. Apparently, you don't need to be a feminist to be attacked; you just need to be a woman speaking in public.

Once I started paying attention, I noticed how many headlines there were about online harassment, how consistently the targets were women, and how little scholarship was available to help me make sense of it. Communications scholar Joseph Reagle notes that most theories of digital toxicity boil down to accounts of "good people acting badly" and "bad people acting out." In the first, theories such as those of disinhibition effects and de-individuation hold that the unique characteristics of the digital environment lead otherwise normal people to behave in abnormal ways. The second formulation, "bad people acting out," suggests that there are a few "bad apples" with particular personality profiles responsible for the ugliness (2015, 94–97). But we don't really see people lashing out at people; we primarily see *men* lashing out at *women,* particularly women from historically marginalized groups. At what cost? This book is born out of my desire to understand how women who want or need to participate in public conversations about political and social issues navigate this menacing landscape, and the ways that this abuse—and women's response to it—shapes political life more broadly.

Digital publics are rife with male resistance to women who participate in public discourse, as we see with Emma Gonzalez. And rather than taking issue with their ideas, the abuse targets their identities, pummeling them with rape threats, attacks on their appearance and presumed sexual behavior, and a cacophony of misogynistic, racist, xenophobic, and homophobic stereotypes and epithets. Gonzalez is challenged for her stance on gun violence, and her race is invoked in the process. Attackers use gendered and homophobic language such as "ugly dyke bitch," "slut," and "cunt," and they cast her in graphic stories of sexual violence. Heated discussion, criticism, and exchange can be uncomfortable, but productive (Papacharissi 2016). This is not that kind of exchange.

Emma Gonzalez is not a participant in this study, but the women I interviewed have also been on the receiving end of identity-based attacks online. For some, the abuse came in response to activism; for others, it emerged in the course of their professional lives as journalists, pundits, academics, or authors. For still others, it is the price they pay for sharing their opinions, expertise, and experiences via editorials, blogs, vlogs, or public social media accounts. This book offers a glimpse into the hostile climate created for these women online, reveals the absence of support structures available for those who seek recourse, and digs deeply into the incredible labor undertaken by women who want or need to stay involved in public conversations about political and social issues. It also excavates the under-explored societal-level costs of identity-based attacks online, showing that when the harassment succeeds in pressing women out of digital spaces, constrains the topics they address publicly, or limits the ways they address them, it has disturbing costs for democracy.

Feminist scholarship has helped to establish that digital misogyny is an extension of the history of attempts to curtail women's freedom to use public spaces as equals (Citron 2014; Filipovic 2007; Franks 2011; Mantilla 2015). This book begins with that assumption; I approach the identity-based vitriol directed at Gonzalez, for example, as attempts to humiliate and discredit her though tried and true forms of resistance to women's presence in spaces men would prefer to control. Like street harassment and sexual harassment in the workplace, digital harassment rejects women's implicit claims to be taken seriously as interlocutors, colleagues, and peers. That is, digital abuse is aimed at protecting and reinforcing a gender system in which women exist primarily as bodies for male evaluation and pleasure. When they weigh in on public issues online, women often find themselves launched into an uncomfortable, yet familiar game of public degradation as sport. Competitors vie to assert dominance and impress their cronies by making the target as uneasy as possible. They seek her degradation, silence, or withdrawal through public conjecture about her physical attributes and sexual desirability. Should this fail to produce the desired effects, they turn to threats of physical violence.

This brand of identity-based abuse can look and feel like interpersonal bullying, but hostility from strangers online is rarely personal. Telling someone she is a filthy whore, for example, is intimate and ad hominem and yet decidedly generic. If we look at the abuse directed at two women from similar social locations, the attacks directed toward them are often interchangeable. We may be able to distinguish the comments, for example, as the kind of abuse pointed at Black women, but be unable to distinguish what they have to do with *any particular* Black woman. This is a reminder; this abuse is structural, rooted in hostility toward the voice and visibility of individual speakers as *representatives* of specific groups of people. The impersonality signals that this phenomenon is a patterned, visceral response to the threat of equality in valued digital conversations and arenas. Recognizing this abuse as patterned resistance rather than interpersonal bullying helps us understand why the attacks are unevenly distributed, tending to increase in frequency and severity for women who have historically been devalued (e.g., women of color) and those whose presence is perceived as especially threatening (e.g., by virtue of their ideas or perceived influence).

Identity-based digital attacks come at great economic, professional, and psychological costs to those who suffer through them, as I will show. But recognizing them as a form of patterned resistance also demands that we confront the societal-level costs of this pointed animosity. We must ask, What if Emma Gonzalez and women like her decide that the price for their political participation and leadership is just too great? What if they stay politically visible, but only share popular opinions on noncontroversial issues? And what do other women learn from watching those denigrated and threatened because they participated in digital discourse? How does the particularly unforgiving response to women of color and/or women from other marginalized groups shape which women "opt" out?

Data and Scope of Research

This book is grounded in four years of in-depth interviews with 52 women who have received identity-based digital abuse from strangers. Although some women in this research have been harassed online by people they know, and intimate digital harassment and abuse such as stalking and cyberbullying emerged in some interviews, the focus of this research and my interviews is on *impersonal* abuse. That is, this book is about digital backlash from strangers (at least, those who appear to be strangers). The women I interviewed speak and write publicly, many as journalists, activists, academics, blog/vloggers, or pundits, and they address issues including science, technology, sex, gaming, sports, violence against women, politics, abortion, racial inequality, and the law. They were attacked on a variety of platforms, from Facebook, Twitter, and YouTube to the comments sections of newspapers and magazines, Tumblr, Reddit, and Instagram. Some of the toxicity is delivered via private messages and emails. The sample includes participants ranging from 19 to 67 years old. Thirty-eight self-identified as white, 14 as women of color. The sample contains both lesbian, gay, bisexual, transgender, and queer (LGBTQ) women and women from religious minority groups. Most, but not all, of the women are based in the United States, with the balance from Canada and Europe (thus their experiences cannot be assumed to represent the experiences of women in other cultural and political contexts). The interviews took place between 2015 and 2019.[1]

Participants have chosen or been assigned pseudonyms, and the excerpts presented here have been carefully redacted to protect their identities. In some cases, I withhold even general information about respondents' careers and/ or the topics on which they are vocal in order to protect their confidentiality. What's more, I focus on participants' experience with and feelings about the attacks waged against them rather than lingering on the substance of the attacks. When I do discuss the content of the abuse, I intentionally provide vague or redacted examples rather than concrete details, as attacks made in public could prove identifying. Any stories or information that *appears* to be identifying is coincidental, made possible only by the unfortunate abundance of women who have dealt with digital abuse and the repetitive nature of the abuse levied against them. In other words, while the insults, threats, and stereotypes described here may sound like wildly similar to the hate lobbed at women readers know personally or have heard about in the news, nothing shared in these pages can be used to identify the participants. It is, however, intellectually worthwhile to note the consistencies.

The interview data are supplemented by extended conversations with professionals working in content moderation, internet safety, and advocacy and have been enriched by my participation in workshops such as the workshop on High Impact Research in Online Harassment and Moderation convened at MIT and the Social Science Research Council workshop on Race, Gender, and Toxicity Online held at the University of Texas. Media coverage of digital sexism was instructive, as was content analytic research on tweets directed at US legislators of varying race and gender I conducted with Shaan Merchant (Sobieraj and Merchant forthcoming).

Digital Publics and Inequities

Internet and communications technologies (ICTs) have been rightly heralded for facilitating a new, more participatory media environment. These ICTs have created important opportunities for people from historically disadvantaged groups, opening the door to a greater diversity of voices in public conversation.[2] Social networking services and user-generated content platforms helped flatten (though did not eliminate) barriers to access—it is easier and far less costly to start a vlog, for instance, than to launch a television network. Participatory online spaces such as comment sections, blogs, Facebook, Twitter, and YouTube now serve as digital public spheres in the sense that they provide a space for and include the practice of open discussion about matters of common concern (Habermas 1991). Such discourse still routinely happens face-to-face, as when we discuss neighborhood issues in community centers, but mass media and online platforms serve as core components of the public sphere in contemporary political culture. Mediated public conversations transpired in legacy media as well, on op-ed pages and through radio call-in programs, for example, but ICTs have supported the proliferation of spaces for public discussion. They even help facilitate what Clay Shirky (2008) refers to as the self-synchronization of latent groups. In other words, these online spaces help people with common interests or attributes find one another, regardless of traditional barriers such as geography and mobility. They reduce coordination costs and collapse distance, in more ways than one (Earl and Kimport 2011; Rohlinger and Bunnage 2017).

Digital publics are of particular import in the context of conventional public spheres, which have always been exclusionary. There has never been equal access to mainstream public spaces, nor have all voices or styles of communication been valued equally when included in the conversation.[3] The micropublics that we find online are new incarnations of the subaltern counter publics valued by Nancy Fraser (1990) and others, who see them as spaces for articulating marginalized interests and viewpoints, building social cohesion, and establishing alternative interpretations of unfolding events and existing social arrangements. What's more, niche publics can serve as staging grounds for the development of strategies to inject marginalized interests and views into mainstream public discourse.[4] To the extent that digital spaces—chat rooms, Twitter networks, Facebook groups, and the like—serve as micropublics, they have the potential to provide safe havens and support for those from marginalized groups and/or with minority viewpoints, facilitating collaboration as participants work to carve out space in mainstream discourse for their issues and voices.[5] Ideally these tools allow users to establish discursive arenas where those whose freedom in public spaces has always been precarious can enter, explore, and share freely. Indeed, such spaces have proven to be valuable sources of solidarity for those from minority groups (Bonilla and Rosa 2015; Keller 2012; Rapp et al. 2010). Of course, whether they prove able to mobilize marginalized participants or to reinforce existing inequalities is an empirical question (Nam 2012; Norris 2001; Park 2013; Schradie 2012). Regardless, we know that these niche publics serve not only as sanctuaries but also as incubators for engagement with outsiders.

"Hashtag activism" is one such form of outreach. For example, people have gathered to call attention to and protest racial inequality by using the #BlackLivesMatter (BLM) hashtag, while outsiders have pushed back, responding and hashtagging their messages with #AllLivesMatter. These efforts did not remain isolated on Twitter. Deen Freelon and his colleagues measured the digital traces of social media activism (e.g., retweets, hashtags, etc.) around the BLM movement over the course of nearly a year, looking at crossover between social media activism and mainstream news coverage. Social media work proved efficacious: the movement's #BlackLivesMatter digital activism predicted mainstream news coverage of police brutality, which proved to be the strongest predictor of attention to the issue from high-ranking elected officials and appointees. The authors note that social movements, "situated within an advanced democracy, led by marginalized but tech-savvy youth, and eager for policy change—may use Twitter to . . . further policy-relevant goals" (Freelon, McIlwain, and Clark 2018, 1006).

But hashtag activism is only one part of the story. Sometimes digital micro-publics are used to launch coordinated efforts offline. Participants work together to reach elected officials, start boycotts, or find co-complainants for class action lawsuits. And at times these geographically dispersed groups coalesce into collective action in the traditional social movement sense, spawning marches and rallies, as seen in the wake of Donald Trump's inauguration (Fisher 2019; Harlow 2012; Boulianne, Koc-Michalska, and Bimber 2020; Tufekci and Wilson 2012).

Perhaps nowhere is the utility of new ICTs for those from disadvantaged groups more apparent than in efforts for cultural visibility. In contrast to efforts that seek legislative or judicial change, campaigns with visibility as their primary end goal are tailor made for this media environment. Social networking services and user-generated content platforms facilitate self-publishing, if not instant distribution (which requires access to a substantial marketing budget, or a combination of skill, persistence, extensive social networks, and serendipity). Having a platform is a start. Occasionally, cultural campaigns capture the attention of conventional media. When this happens, activists' reach can be extended exponentially via print, TV, and radio outlets. The hashtag #OscarsSoWhite provides one excellent example. It first appeared online in 2015, drawing attention to racial imbalances in Hollywood. By 2016, the hashtag was being featured by myriad traditional news outlets. The hashtag and frame #OscarsSoWhite, still figured prominently in discussions about nominations, presenters, and awardees in 2020. Digital publics, therefore, can provide alternatives and paths to mainstream news coverage.

The spheres of publicity made available via digital life radically improve access to information for those at the margins and create new platforms from which to speak. Still, the entrenched inequalities we find offline—such as the hierarchies of race, class, gender, sexual orientation, ability, and national origin—reappear in and across digital arenas. Barriers to entry may be lower, but access to and legitimacy within digital public spaces remain unequal. And the digital production gap—unequal involvement in content creation—has been particularly resilient (Schradie 2011; 2015). Even when digital publics include a diversity of participants, inequities shape their comfort, involvement, and social power (Herring 1999; 1996; Milner 2012).

Gender Inequality Online

Despite some early imaginings that new ICTs would liberate women by allowing them to transcend gender and disrupt patriarchal arrangements (Braidotti 2003; Haraway 1987; Plant 1997), new technologies are neither universally liberating nor oppressive (Daniels 2009b). Instead, technologies—digital and otherwise—are social constructions that are malleable, context dependent, and open to interpretation. Further, technology and gender are not separate entities but are rather co-produced, leading Judy Wajcman to describe technology as "a source and consequence of gender relations" (2004; 2010, 148). Newer ICTs, like their predecessors, are new arenas in which gender inequities are recreated, reformed, and resisted.

These gender inequalities take a variety of forms. Some digital communities are androcentric, informally excluding women by creating an unwelcoming climate (Kendall 2002; Herring 1996; Martin et al. 2015; Reagle 2013; Turkle 1984). Much of this androcentrism is overt (e.g., Dignam and Rohlinger 2019), though it can also be subtle—accomplished by overvaluing men's input and expertise while devaluing women's (e.g., Korn 2015). In some instances, familiar physical forms of violence against women, such as stalking, sexual harassment, and sexual assault, are facilitated by ICTs. This digital component often heightens the suffering experienced by victims. Think, for example, about the ways digital documentation of rape and sexual assault re-traumatize survivors through public shaming and humiliation facilitated by sharing technologies (Henry and Powell 2015).[6] Regardless, women, particularly women of color, bear the brunt of digital hate—freely flung insults, threats, and abuse, much of which is shamelessly misogynistic, racist, xenophobic, and heterosexist (Amnesty International 2018; Gardiner 2018; Döring and Mohseni 2018; Phillips 2015; Citron 2014; Herring et al. 2002; Herring 2002; Jane 2014b; Filipovic 2007; Gray 2014; Sills et al. 2016; Pintak et al. 2019; Sobieraj 2019; Finn 2004).

Understanding digital attacks as fundamentally entwined with power and inequality helps us understand why identity-based abuse is unevenly distributed *among* women. I find the attacks are particularly severe for (1) women who are members of multiple marginalized groups, (2) those who are speaking publicly in or about male-dominated spheres, and (3) women who are perceived as feminist or noncompliant with traditional gender norms. Of course, these categories are not mutually exclusive, as illustrated in Figure I.1.

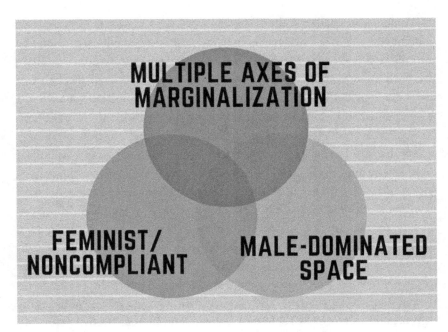

Figure I.1 Attributes of Women Targeted by Particularly Severe Digital Attacks

Drawing on the core conceptual work on intersectionality by Kimberle Crenshaw (1989), we can see that identity-based attacks against women reflect the broader, interlocking systems of inequality and oppression in which attackers and targets are embedded. As a result, digital abuse is unusually burdensome for women of color—particularly Black women—(Amnesty International 2018; Gray 2012; 2014; Madden et al. 2018), but it is also qualitatively different from the kinds of abuse directed at White women or Black men. Black women, for example, receive gender—and race-based—attacks, but also racialized gender-based attacks that deploy the specific stereotypes and myths that have historically been used to pathologize them. What's more, the experiences among Black women are further shaped by complex stratifying matrices of advantage and disadvantage such as those of class, ethnicity, religion, citizenship, and sexuality. Throughout this book, when I speak about harassment and abuse directed at "women," it is with full knowledge that there is immense internal variation among women not only in the amount and kind of abuse they navigate but also in its impact (see Chapter 4 for a discussion of the role of privilege in coping).[7]

Women who challenge the norms and practices in arenas that are male dominated, such as science, technology, gaming, sports, politics, finance, and the military, also receive a tremendous amount of backlash (Antunovic 2019; Everbach 2018; Gardiner 2018). These women may intentionally challenge the status quo in these circles, by pointing out discrimination, but when a woman enters a space that is male-dominated and expects to be taken seriously, her mere presence is often interpreted as a challenge, regardless of intent.

Another group of women who are frequently harassed online are feminist or otherwise noncompliant with gender norms are often subject vicious attack (e.g., Eckert 2018). I use the term noncompliant broadly to capture an array of women, not only those who self-identify publicly as feminists. These can include, for example, women holding positions of power, women being open about enjoying sex, and women who have the audacity to be both overweight and body positive. Gender-based harassment, both online and off, is a way to punish women who violate gender norms and reassert their boundaries (Maass et al. 2003; Berdahl 2007; Holland and Cortina 2013; McLaughlin, Uggen, and Blackstone 2012; Siebler, Sabelus, and Bohner 2008).

Returning to the case of Emma Gonzalez, we can locate her right in the center of the Venn diagram from Figure I.1. First, her social identities combine, making her subject to multiple modes of oppression; Gonzalez is female, but she is also Latinx—appearing in front of the cameras with a Cuban flag on her jacket—and bisexual (though often presumed lesbian). She is also decidedly noncompliant with traditional gender norms by virtue of both her rage (female victims are expected to cry, not "call BS") and her appearance (her shaved head, in particular). Finally, Gonzalez's political fury is trained on guns and gun laws, a historically male province. Emma Gonzalez is a destabilizer. She is, to borrow a term, a triple threat. The dehumanizing backlash directed at her reflects the dis-ease her voice and visibility create.

Male hostility toward women who cross boundaries is not, of course, unique to digital life. In considering the digital abuse leveled at feminists, particularly her own harassment on the law school rumor mill board AutoAdmit and that experienced by Amanda Marcotte and Melissa McEwan while they worked for John Edwards's 2008 presidential campaign, Jill Filipovic underscores the ways that internet misogyny parallels gendered harassment in physical spaces. She suggests that the heart of men's aggression toward women is a "generalized offense at women's public presence in 'men's' spaces—in politics, at law schools, online" (2007, 298). This parallels the experiences of women in the workplace, who face pronounced sexual harassment when they are in positions of authority and/or in male-dominated employment contexts such as the military, law enforcement, and construction (Dresden et al. 2018; McLaughlin, Uggen, and Blackstone 2012; Kabat-Farr and Cortina 2014; Konik and Cortina 2008; Magley et al. 1999; see also Welsh 1999 for a review).

It is unsurprising, then, that the risk of unwanted sexual attention and violence have long constrained women's use of public space. Whether through the fear of sexual assault that looms over women as they navigate the world (Clark 2015; Wesely and Gaarder 2004; Roper 2016), the sense of vulnerability and humiliation that accompany street harassment (Fairchild and Rudman 2008; Gardner 1995; Miller 2008; Nielsen 2004), or the labyrinthine challenges presented by sexual harassment in the workplace (Williams, Giuffre, and Dellinger 1999; Sojo, Wood, and Genat 2016; Welsh 1999; McLaughlin, Uggen, and Blackstone 2012), women's freedom, comfort, and safety are curtailed by the threat of gender-based intimidation and violence. Men from marginalized groups, particularly men of color and queer people of all races, are also well versed in the calculus of risk.

Over 30 years ago, geographer Gill Valentine documented how women constrained their use of public space based on mental maps they constructed based on their fear of male violence. The sense of danger impeded women's independence and freedom; it shaped where they went, at what times, and with whom. Valentine concluded: "This cycle of fear becomes one subsystem by which male dominance, patriarchy, is maintained and perpetuated" (1989, 389). I find that the fear engendered by patterned hostility toward women's presence in digital publics has similar consequences. Just as inhibited use of physical public spaces is a spatial expression of gender-based oppression, inhibited use of comment sections, social media platforms, blogs, vlogs, and online gaming must be understood as its digital expression.

Identity-Based Attacks against Women Online

In listening to women's accounts and watching digital harassment unfold, I find that aggressors repeatedly draw on three overlapping strategies to limit women's impact in digital publics: intimidating, shaming, and discrediting. With intimidation, attackers draw on women's fear of rape and physical violence. Public shaming attempts regularly exploit double standards about women's sexual behavior and physical appearance to smear their targets. And efforts to discredit often employ sexist stereotypes to devalue women and their contributions. These three tactics are deeply entwined and not mutually exclusive, but I address them separately for analytic purposes.

Attackers often try to *intimidate*. Intimidation appears in threats of physical violence, such as death and rape threats, which abound, as well as in intimations that the attacker knows where the person lives or works and vague but frightening suggestions that the target should shut up lest their families come to harm. Sometimes denial of service (DOS) and distributed denial of service (DDOS) attacks are used to make the target feel vulnerable and to effectively, if temporarily, restrict her access to the web (or a particular website), slow network performance, or bombard her email account with spam. "Swatting" is another, albeit far less common, intimidation tactic, in which attackers make false emergency calls to the police indicating that there is an imminent threat at the target's location (e.g., a hostage situation, a bomb threat, or an active shooter). The goal is to terrify the target when a SWAT team descends on her. Although swatting is often referred to as a prank, the label belies the gravity of the experience. As writer Joe Fagone described in the *New York Times*,

> K. says she opened the door of her Florida apartment one evening to find a dozen SWAT officers lined up on the stairs with riot shields and black guns pointed at her. She froze and thought of the metal belt buckle she happened to be clutching in her left hand. "They're going to think I have a weapon in my hand. They're going to shoot me." (Fagone 2016)

"Doxxing" (a reference to "dropping documents"), in which attackers compile personal information about a target and publish it without her consent with the intent of enticing other harassers, is another intimidation tactic. One of the participants in this research who had been the subject of an intense wave of digital hostility, described her horror in discovering that her home address, the floor plans to her house, photos of her car, and other personal information had all been published online. Such efforts escalate the fear of physical violence by implying (and making more feasible) that threats made online might translate into physical violence. Doxxing can also involve revealing the identity of a previously anonymous person. This helps us see how closely linked and overlapping the three tactics of aggression can be: threatening to dox is perhaps best understood as intimidation, but when it exposes someone's identity, it is often also used to shame or discredit.

Attacks against women online often involve attempts to publicly *shame* them. Missives drawing on public shame strive to contaminate the public perception of the target. The most notorious of these tactics is the circulation of nonconsensual pornography (NCP): this includes posting nude or otherwise compromising photos or videos, originally taken with an understanding that they would remain private (often obtained through hacking or via former intimate partners) as well as those taken without consent, such as those captured by hidden cameras or while the target was incapacitated. These images need not even need be real for them to function as devices for shaming. For example, four participants in this research reported that attackers edited their faces onto degrading or violent pornographic images and circulated them. When combined with doxxing, unauthorized and falsified sexual images humiliate the target and open the floodgates to an onslaught of digital harassment.

Of course, this is not the only attempt by attackers to shame women. Harassers sometimes seek to shame their targets by disclosing private information, often de- or mis-contextualizing the details for maximum impact. Public shame attempts may also involve circulating patently false information that attackers hope others will find reprehensible (e.g., making allegations about her sexual history) and/or making efforts to recast public actions in a markedly negative light. Regardless of the methods used, shaming tactics are distinctive in the way they attempt to take control of how the target is perceived in an effort to humiliate or—as is often the goal—discredit her.

Efforts to *discredit* women are extremely common online. These dispatches regularly draw on gender-based stereotypes that suggest the target cannot possibly have anything worthwhile to contribute or that she is not a credible source. Often she is described as incapable of an unbiased opinion or perspective because she is a bitch, a ditz, emotional, needs to get laid, a dumb blonde, a whore, or suffering from PMS (premenstrual syndrome), to offer a few examples. In many cases, attackers suggest that her personal accounts, political views, or concerns about social arrangements can't be taken seriously because their target has an ulterior motive (e.g. she is a gold digger, a feminazi, or a "social justice warrior"). The stereotypes invoked to discredit vary based on the identity of the target, often stamped by attributes such as racism, classism, or xenophobia. So, for example, it is not uncommon to see discrediting attempts against Black women that draw on stereotypes such as the angry Black woman and the welfare queen. As a mode of attack, these identity-based stereotypes strive to devalue the knowledge, opinions, and experiences of those under fire.

This is what resistance to women's voice and visibility looks like.

Understanding the Centrality of Women's Bodies

Gender is both motive and means when it comes to digital harassment. Gender shapes the propensity of a person to be an attacker or a target, but gender is also at the center of the attacks themselves. Whether they are working to intimidate, shame, or discredit their mark, when people (mostly men) lash out at women, they use their femaleness against them. In other words, gender is implicated in the tools that are used to attack, not only in the actors who use them. Women with visibility are often deluged with vitriolic tweets, emails, and comments that draw on sexist name-calling, negative stereotypes, double standards, and sexual objectification. Vocativ analyzed 80,000 tweets directed at broadcaster Megyn Kelly's Twitter handle over the 24-hour period after Donald Trump announced that he would not participate in a televised debate she was moderating. In that brief window, tweets directed at Kelly included the words bitch (n = 423), bimbo (n = 404), blonde (n = 128), whore (n = 88), cheap (n = 66), ugly (n = 59), skank (n = 39), cunt (n = 34), slut (n = 27), and hooker (n = 13) (Cuen and Evers 2016). The language is explicitly gender-based, dominated by misogynistic epithets, evaluations of her sexual value, and sexist stereotypes (e.g., the dumb blonde).

Substantive commentary is noticeably absent. Potentially relevant journalistic critiques, assertions that Kelly is "biased," "unfair," or "hostile," for example, are drowned out by reminders that she is a woman and thus without value or that she is the *kind* of woman who has no value. Kelly's alleged sexual behavior and physical appearance, which have nothing to do with her skills as a moderator, become the central grounds for condemnation. This is indicative of a broader pattern in which a woman's physical appearance and sexual propriety are treated as universally relevant. It is particularly noteworthy that no evidence is offered to support these claims; the allegation alone is treated as reason to view Kelly with contempt.

All of this evokes the anecdotal "feedback" directed at Emma Gonzalez. The tweets with which I opened this chapter incorporated misogynistic epithets, such as "cunt" and "bitch," and also included references to her physical appearance and sexual behavior (she was called "ugly," "absolutely revolting," and a "slut," for example). Still others drew on sexist stereotypes, such as one in which she is described as a "drama queen," or, for context, an "UGLY SKINHEAD FREAKSHOW DRAMA QUEEN."

As I read unsettling examples of identity-based attacks against women detailed by scholars such as Emma Jane (2014a), Danielle Citron (2014), Joanne Garde-Hansen, and Kristyn Gorton (2013) and listen to the stories shared by my participants, I am struck by their vulgarity, cruelty, and violence. But I am also struck by the way they so pointedly use women's bodies as leverage. A preponderance of the instances incorporate one or more of the following: rape threats or graphic descriptions of sexual torture; commentary about the person's presumed sexual behavior (e.g., whore, slut, prude) and physical appearance (often amounting to whether the woman in question is even "worth raping"); racialized remarks about their bodies or presumed sexual utility; seething speculations about their sexual orientation, preferences, or fetishes; use of the c-word; descriptions of nonsexual violence or torture; use of pornographic imagery; use of doctored images of the target (often sexualized and humiliating); the circulation of unauthorized sexually explicit images—it goes on. Regardless of what women do or say before they are attacked, their bodies take center stage in the abuse.

The long history of women's objectification and sexualization is not only about sexual desire and the exertion of power but also about laying the groundwork that is fundamental to defining and reestablishing what it means to be a member of a particular sex category. Legal scholar Reva Siegel notes, for example, that sexual harassment in the workplace "engenders as it coerces" and is part of a "practice that 'makes' women and men men" (2003, 17). The assertion that sex difference (alongside other differences) is essential and immutable benefits those whose positions in the social hierarchy imbue them with value. The cultural baggage we append to those perceived as inhabiting these different categories likewise gives weight to certain groups' attributes, ideas, labors, and forms of expression. Objectification and sexualization, in the context of digital sexism, are much the same: they are about desire, power, norms, and inequalities, but this dominance work becomes more challenging in the absence of a physically co-present body. Through this lens, it makes sense that bodily references would be especially valuable, indeed omnipresent, in computer mediated communications—they help reinforce the salience of gender in the digital arena.[8]

Research suggests that computer mediated communication reduces status inequality precisely because we have a smaller number of available social cues with which to assess our interlocutors. When we interact online, we have fewer markers of race, age, gender, class, level of education, sexual orientation, ethnicity, religion, and ability—particularly in text-based exchanges.

The "equalization hypothesis" suggests that there is a leveling effect in digital exchanges. Proponents argue that this makes computer mediated interactions somewhat more equitable than face-to-face communications. We often feel and communicate *as though* we are on a more even footing when we enter digital arenas (Bordia 1997; Boucher, Hancock, and Dunham 2008; Dubrovsky, Kiesler, and Sethna 1991; George et al. 1990). Groups accustomed to having the upper hand, those who are usually presumed credible, important, or authoritative by default, are unlikely to appreciate this recalibration.

Gender permeates our lives online, but digital arenas preclude some of the physical strategies men use to control interactions and to display dominance in the face-to-face exchanges. Differences in physical stature, for example, that often advantage men are not relevant in digital exchanges, nor can men rely on commanding body postures, nonverbal gestures that signal dominance (e.g., invasive touch), or communicative habits such as interruption or amplification to maximize their influence and command attention. More overt tactics for exerting influence, such as physical intimations that suggest the threat of violence and the exploitation of power differentials emerging from employment or position, are also less relevant to comment sections, chat rooms, and the world of online games. As a result, the unspoken and often unrecognized communicative advantages of masculinity in social interaction are subtly destabilized in digital publics. This is likely to feel particularly disorienting in spaces with a history (however short) of being predominantly male or that focus on topics that are usually the province of men, in which (consciously or not) men feel that their opinions, ideas, and insights should carry the day.[9]

I am convinced that these sexist missives take the form of body-based commentary because talking about women's bodies—about their sexuality, appearance, or physical vulnerability—is a shortcut that works to force gender into the conversation. They can be understood as flailing attempts to reassert the centrality of gender difference—and the gender inequality that comes with it—in spaces where its grip, though powerful, may feel feebler. Such gender billboards are important in digital arenas: Tim Jordan writes, "Online markers of identity—because they are inherently unstable, unlike the body or timbre of a voice—have to be stabilized by being heard consistently" (Shepherd et al. 2015, 3). These perseverations on the female body seek to achieve this stabilization. They announce femaleness, but, of course, not only femaleness. When the woman is a member of other historically devalued identity groups, aggressors insert those markers of unworthiness into the backlash as well. In this way, we can see these body-centric attacks for what they are: adjacent, yet not equivalent, to practices such as outing and othering that also serve to ensure that difference is rendered salient and therefore available to use as leverage. As Lois McNay reminds us, gender is accomplished through lived social relations that are negotiated and renegotiated (2004). That the locus of attack is the body is thus instrumental rather than coincidental. Words such as cunt, dyke, and whore sound the alarm. They shout: "This is a woman." "You are a woman." "She is a woman." They communicate: "This is unimportant." "You are unimportant." "She is unimportant."

The Costs of Identity-Based Attacks against Women Online

Public harassment has long been a geographic expression of social inequality and an effective means for dominant groups to maintain control of communal spaces. Street and sexual harassment are nearly universal experiences for women, particularly Black and Latina women and poor women of all races and ethnicities (Gardner 1995; Miller 2008; Nielsen 2004). And while women certainly continue to use public space, research shows that they constrain their behaviors in response to prior experiences with harassment and the fear of sexual intimidation and violence (Gardner 1995; Hollander 2001; Fairchild and Rudman 2008; Meyer and Grollman 2014; Riger and Gordon 1981; Wesely and Gaarder 2004). Indeed, Carol Brooks Gardner (1995) highlights that harassment inhibits women's use of public space, *even when no harassment transpires*. Fear of harassment diminishes women's comfort and freedom, acting as a form of oppression.

Women strategize their way around uncomfortable and frightening public spaces when they can, to avoid the threat of male violence and sexual intimidation. They make the mental maps described by Valentine (1989). Where is it safe to go? When is it safe to be there? How should I behave to minimize the likelihood of harassment? How will I react if something it happens? Women of privilege have more options. More affluent women may be able to avoid communities and workplaces they find threatening. Or they may be able to drive, take a taxi, or even hire a lawyer or bodyguard as protective measures. But all women operate with an awareness of the looming possibility of unwanted attention when entering public space.

The threat of abuse is increasingly part of the digital landscape women navigate. Not all women who speak in digital spaces are attacked, but Chapter 1 will take readers into the hostile speaking environment faced by many. Women's stories help map the range of digital pushback from the commonplace (starting their days with misogynistic insults in their inboxes or the comments on their social media posts) to the life-altering (receiving coordinated death and rape threats such as those that compelled Dr. Christine Blasey Ford to go into hiding after testifying against US Supreme Court nominee Brett Kavanaugh). This chapter also shows that attacks vary in intensity and substance, and explores the way that attackers targeting women from marginalized groups weaponize their race, religion, sexual orientation, and other devalued identities into venomous intersectional abuse.

Chapter 2 untangles the way that digital abuse against women is trivialized by employers, law enforcement, and even well-intentioned loved ones. Further, it lays bare the way that even those under fire minimize and normalize their experiences. With Chapter 1, it demonstrates that most women who are attacked online have little recourse, and sometimes eschew what recourse *is* available because they have internalized the same set of trivializing myths, even if they understand them to be inaccurate. Chapters 3 and 4 highlight the time-consuming and exhausting work of battling digital attacks, from the backflips women do in an effort to avoid harassment to the strategies they use to cope once the onslaught has begun. Many women use and relish digital platforms, but it is not difficult to imagine why they adopt real-world tactics to navigate around high-risk online spaces.

In Chapter 5, I show the toll digital misogyny has taken on the women in this research. It has cost some of my participants their jobs, forced them to change their place of residence, jeopardized their mental health, placed them at risk of physical violence, and caused irreparable reputational damage in keeping with other research (Bates 2017; Barak 2005; Citron 2014). Some women, even without overt threat, decide that the constant irritation and inconvenience is too tedious to tolerate; sifting through the barrage of sexist hostility to find the more meaningful responses, becoming upset by venomous screeds, or needing to block and report people on social media services is a weight that is difficult to carry. In this sense, to "opt out" of digital life is similar to what scholars have found about women "opting out" of other spheres of life: it is far less about opting out than being forced out. The difference is in degree, not kind.

That is to say, Chapter 5 shows that when effective, identity-based attacks silence women, undermine their contributions to digital discourse, create a climate of self-censorship, and in the most concerning cases, press them out of digital publics altogether. We will see that even the boldest and most resilient women rely on mental maps to guide them, if imperfectly, through a digital landscape they know is dangerous for destabilizers. This chapter then explores the rarely examined and deeply worrisome democratic costs of identity-based attacks online that exist alongside the personal ones, showing that the specter of digital misogyny erodes free speech and limits the diversity of speakers and ideas composing our democratic discourse. The hostile speaking environment and lack of structural response to digital misogyny taxes even those who are not directly involved.

It is essential, but no small feat, to create structural solutions to prevent and ameliorate patterned resistance to women's visibility. I conclude the book with a call for structural solutions, examine existing legal approaches, and explore emerging attempts to hold platforms accountable. I also ask policymakers to add victim-centered support structures to their agenda alongside emerging perpetrator- and platform-focused remedies. It is my hope that this work will pave the way for new, stronger efforts to support robust inclusivity in digital spaces.

1

Hostile Speaking Environment

In her rich exploration of the history of workplace sexual harassment in the United States, Reva Siegel revisits the gender integrations of the 1970s and 1980s. She shows that these symbolically significant transitions were met with resistance: "Sexualized attention emerged as a weapon in this turf war, a means of making women feel so unwelcome that they would eventually leave" (2003, 19). Long before the language of "opting out," women were being driven out of spaces and opportunities that had recently opened to them. Men used a varied repertoire of techniques to undermine women's inclusion in traditionally male workplaces (that is to say, the majority of them). In addition to unwanted sexual attention, resistance to women's full incorporation in the workplace also came in the form of uncomfortable interactions that were concurrently nonsexual and yet fundamentally about sex and gender. Male colleagues learned to call out sex and gender—by doing things such as telling sexist jokes or using belittling gendered nicknames such "sweetheart" or "doll"—as a way to highlight the abnormality of women's presence, in so doing, they degraded and ridiculed both specific women and broader social shifts toward equality. Their comments and behaviors made it clear: only men truly belong.

In 1986, the US Supreme Court ruled that discrimination on the basis of sex created a hostile and abusive work environment in violation of Title VII of the Civil Rights Act of 1964. As per the EEOC website:

> Harassment becomes unlawful where 1) enduring the offensive conduct becomes a condition of continued employment, or 2) the conduct is severe or pervasive enough to create a work environment that a reasonable person would consider intimidating, hostile, or abusive. . . . To be unlawful, the conduct must create a work environment that would be intimidating, hostile, or offensive to reasonable people.

Credible Threat. Sarah Sobieraj, Oxford University Press (2020). © Oxford University Press.
DOI: 10.1093/oso/9780190089283.001.0001.

Plaintiffs bringing hostile work environment suits under Title VII must demonstrate that others' conduct in the workplace was severe or pervasive, created a hostile or abusive working environment, was unwelcome, and was based on their gender. This is a fruitful way to think about speech environments as well as working environments. If we replace the words "employment" and "work" with "public speech" and "speaking," we find an apt description of the digital environs many women navigate. These descriptors are also used in the 2002 Directive on Equal Treatment issued by the European Union (EU), which defines sexual harassment as

> any form of unwanted verbal, non-verbal or physical conduct of a sexual nature with the purpose or effect of violating the dignity of a person, in particular when creating an intimidating, hostile, degrading, humiliating or offensive environment.

The two definitions differ in important ways: most significantly, the EU definition is written from the victim's point of view, while in the United States a (presumably unaffiliated) "reasonable person" is designated as the arbiter (Zippel 2006). In spite of these differences, three descriptors resurface across these two widely used interpretations: intimidating, hostile, and offensive.

Debbie, Lynnette, and Fatima

Women's experiences with digital attacks vary, but *intimidating, hostile,* and *offensive* are apt descriptors of the climate navigated by the women I interviewed for this project. Consider, for example, what it might feel like to operate in the speaking environments that Debbie, Lynette, and Fatima inhabit.

Debbie is an intense White woman in her 40s whose tough, sardonic manner suggests she has seen it all. She is an activist and political pundit who serves as the executive director of a nonprofit organization promoting social equality. Debbie has dealt with online harassment for as long as she can remember, going back to her earliest experiences with online gaming. Today, she shares her expertise and opinions on issues related to gender and race on platforms such as Twitter and Facebook and is a talking head on news analysis shows airing on Fox and MSNBC (segments that are often shared and re-shared via social media). Debbie matter-of-factly described how she is assailed by every conceivable gendered epithet, regularly sent pornography, and belittled with gendered stereotypes, especially references to her being a "dumb blonde." Some of the nastiness is not explicitly gendered: one stranger sent photos of his anus, while another created memes about her drinking bleach. But the majority of the abuse drips with overt misogyny. Debbie told me almost nonchalantly,

> I get rape threats. . . . There have been dozens of them. . . . I remember doing a show where I was talking about Iran and . . . this man saying "I'm going to kidnap you and when the Mullahs are done with you you're going to have to wear a diaper." Stuff like that.

Stuff like that.

Lynette is successful, incisive, charming, and exhausted. She is a Black public intellectual in her 30s who writes about social issues for several national publications, publishes books, tweets avidly, blogs, and periodically appears on national television and radio. Lynnette's trenchant social analyses and down-to-earth candor have won her readers and fans from around the world. Her impressive reach and visibility have been accompanied by a stunning amount of hate (she described it as a "tsunami"). Lynette is no stranger to finding overtly racist and misogynistic remarks and pornographic images in her @ mentions, inboxes, and direct messages. The familiarity does not make it less tedious, she explained, "There's just some days where . . . I'm just not going to be a 'nigger bitch' again today." Lynette notes that many who lash out at her are incensed because she is taken seriously as an expert. As a Black woman, she is out of line. Uppity. Seething with rage and bent on discrediting her, attackers challenge her intelligence and authority; they question her credentials. Even the death threats Lynnette receives (there have been many) often make her head the target of their rage. They say they want to bash her head in or shoot her brains out. Attackers have gone further, attempting to destroy her reputation by sending hostile content about her to others. One persistent attacker harvested photos of Lynette's face from her professional sites and edited them onto others' nude photos. He then uploaded them to a nonconsensual pornography website, reached out to her colleagues, and directed them to the doctored pornographic images: the "evidence" she is a fraud.

Fatima is a passionate and accomplished freelance journalist, but not a typical one. She covers a heavily male-dominated beat as a woman of South Asian descent, an observant Muslim, and a feminist. With her outsider's eye and social justice orientation, Fatima often writes articles that address social inequalities in the field, a rarity in this particular arena. Abuse peppers the comment sections of Fatima's stories, the replies she receives on social media, and the email she encounters on any given day. Fatima told me that she's become accustomed to being called an "ugly bitch" and a "feminazi," but as with Lynette, the abuse directed at her is often intersectional. Much of the venom directed at her invokes her ethnicity, perceived national origin, and religion in addition to her gender. Men have sent Fatima "hijab porn," painted grim descriptions of her being stoned to death "where she comes from," and suggested that her hijab be used as a noose. One commenter suggested that her son was a terrorist, even in utero: "It's a good thing the grenade in his hand didn't explode when it came down your pussy."

Like Debbie, Lynette, and Fatima, each of the women I spoke with described navigating speech environments that would be found *hostile* and *offensive* by a "reasonable person," in the language of the Equal Employment Opportunity Commission (EEOC). These digital landscapes are also *intimidating* in two ways. First, they intimidate by provoking fear of physical harm. For example, on two different occasions, men who lashed out at Debbie online have shown up at her workplace unannounced. Another attacker, with a background in information technology, gained access to the audio on her laptop and was able to eavesdrop on her. As a result of numerous death and rape threats, Debbie walks to her car with an emergency app open on her phone. She has had a panic button installed in her office.

In addition to the fear of physical harm, digital attacks generate fear of further digital abuse. Fatima is often fraught with worry about what might come in response to sharing her work online. She calls it *"crippling."* As an illustration, she described a time when a man she blocked on Twitter sent her a detailed email describing having raped a 12-year-old child. Fatima was so disturbed by the content that she vomited. The days that followed left her questioning whether she could muster the energy to continue writing online at this price of admission. This is a hostile speaking environment.

As I mentioned in the Introduction, one of the peculiar things about identity-based abuse is that the attacks, while humiliating and painful, also tend to be generic. They are largely *im*personal and could be brushed across anyone with a similar social location, such that the slurs and threats become nearly interchangeable. And though it may seem odd to describe ad hominem attacks as *impersonal*, spending time in this space quickly lays bare the truth: these attacks are often scathing and vulgar, and they feel like intimate affronts, but they are less about one individual and more about the class of people or type of person the target individual is seen as representing. This boilerplate quality is parodied by Australian scholars Emma Jane and Nicole Vincent who built the "Random Rape Threat Generator" (see Jane 2018 for details). The Random Rape Threat Generator is a digital slot machine with three wheels that spin independently, each containing misogynistic commentary culled from an archive of actual attacks against women online. When users press "play," the spinning wheels stop one at a time, combining to yield a compound insult. My most recent spin generated: "Hope you get raped to death" + "you PC" + "cumdumpster." The tool makes an important point: the hate directed at women online *feels* deeply personal, but most of the comments are rubber-stamped misogyny, adjusted to capture the subject's devalued identities, yet divorced from the behaviors, ideas, or attributes of any particular woman. The anti-Muslim sexism hurled at Fatima could be hurled at any Muslim woman.

Consistency across individual attacks does not mean, of course, that the hostile speaking environment is monolithic. These hostile climates, much like the ones we speak about in the workplace, are multitudinous and varied. As we do offline, we enter multiple speaking cultures online. In some, we feel valued, respected, and safe to share our ideas. In others, we learn to fear judgment or expect hostility. The comment sections of different magazines, blogs, and newspapers vary, as do those within platforms such as Twitter, Tumblr, Facebook, and YouTube.

And the inhabitants of these terrains do not treat all women who enter in a similar way. Even in these brief snapshots of Debbie, Lynnette, and Fatima we can see how the abuse shapes to the perceived identities of the target— latching onto and calling out to those who are devalued. Reflecting on how attackers can cram anti-Semitism, homophobia, and sexism all into a single tweet, Jan, a White lesbian respondent, quipped, "Trolls are nothing if not intersectional." Another form of variation appears in the temporal experience of online attacks. Some of the women I spoke with experienced digital abuse as an ever-present ringing in their ears, something they have learned to live with but cannot fully tune out. Some have been targeted with more intense and episodic fury. And still others have had their lives disrupted by a single profound onslaught, then struggled to rebuild.

Worse than the Sum of Its Parts

Most of the women in this research find it hard to explain their experiences with digital toxicity to those who have not been targeted, because the discrete jabs, epithets, and threats coalesce into an amorphous whole that is more affecting than the sum of its parts. Cat, a contemplative White sports analyst in her 20s, became disillusioned by the tedium of unsolicited comments about her appearance and constant attempts to delegitimate her work. She was frustrated that while outsiders might be able to see examples of the gendered mistreatment she had to deal with, they couldn't fully grasp her day-to-day survival in such toxic spaces:

> I remember a couple of years ago, seeing a video where a team of scientists had put together this series of electro-whatever-pads that they put on a couple of men, so the men could experience the pain of childbirth. And, at first, they were like, "This is fine." By the end, they were astounded. I think if men were, if they experienced the overwhelming aspect to which being a woman online is dictated by gender, if they experienced not only the most tangible evidence of it, the reprisals from random men, sometimes from prominent men, from other women for being a bad example of a woman online. Also, if they experienced the fact that as a result of being a woman in general, we're taught to spend a lot more time composing what we're going to say. We tone-police ourselves. I think those things are . . . insidious and built up over time . . . simply doing that experiment where you throw someone in and say, "You're going to use a female photo and a female name, now go and be on the internet and see how it works." It just doesn't encompass the magnitude of what it means.

The "magnitude of what it means" speaks to the climate as something more significant and pervasive than any set of examples or experiences can fully capture. In this culture, the potential for identity-based attacks and harassment is omnipresent, looming as both latent danger and tedious inconvenience. When Lynette said, "There's just some days where . . . I'm just not going to be a 'nigger bitch' again today," she was not describing any one particular comment but a pattern of comments that have weighed on her over time. Lynette must brace herself daily, because toxicity hovers around the platforms where she communicates. Like Cat, she feels outsiders are unable to understand what it means to be in the crosshairs:

> I think when we say we're harassed, people think, "Oh, somebody said something mean one time." I'm not sure people get the scale,

the frequency, the persistence of people who need to harass you. I don't think they get that. Men clearly do not, most men I know anyway, they clearly don't. They know how to give lip service, like, "Oh, yeah. That's horrible. That's terrible." We've all been now socialized enough we can all perform some type of feminism. "Oh, yeah, yeah, yeah, that's terrible. That's horrible." Like, "No. Can you imagine if right now, when you walked out of the room, I called twenty people over so we could talk about how to destroy your sense of self? That's what is happening. That's what people want. Can you imagine that?" They can't. . . . [U]ntil people can imagine it, they'll keep being super dismissive.

Sophia is a business news editor for the digital arm of a major television network. She is White, in her 30s, and has a background in reporting that introduced her to digital sexism. To her, the gendered hostility is a blur, so voluminous it has become indistinct. A few instances stand out, but it's the overall tenor that she finds noteworthy. Sophia describes people constantly trying to "undercut [female reporters'] worth, based on gender" with sexualizing language, condescending treatment (such as being called "little girl"), and gendered epithets. She described it vividly as "like living in a word cloud" of misogyny.

There are three primary ways that identity-based attacks transform into a larger, more pervasive and impactful climate: They engender an anticipatory fear that more abuse could come at any time, extending the reach of the hostility that has already surfaced. They often lack contextual information about the aggressor or that person's state of mind, leaving recipients in risk-assessment limbo, uncertain if they are responding appropriately. And thanks to mobile technologies, they can be invasive, like an unwelcome visitor who drops by unexpectedly.

THE OTHER SHOE

Even during hostility-free moments, many women who have been attacked online feel as though they are waiting for the other shoe to drop. This is even true for stalwarts of public speech like Esther. Esther is feminist media critic in her 40s who describes herself as White multi-ethnic. She is a prolific author, churning out well-reviewed books and think pieces for national outlets while also working as a key player in feminist advocacy. Smart, savvy, and determined, she liaises seamlessly among women's organizations, policy-makers, academics, and major corporations in her efforts to promote global gender equality. Having been targeted by digital abuse for years, Esther is a veteran, but she says that one of the "costs" of her work is living with a diffuse sense of worry, because it is hard to know what will trigger an attack. Her unease is often preemptive:

> I wrote an article for [a major national newsmagazine] last week. It was about White male dominance, which is very difficult for some people. I had a lot of anxiety writing that, because I was anticipating—which hasn't happened, thank goodness—a really horrible online backlash. I never can predict when it's going to happen or not.

Although the "horrible online backlash" failed to materialize in this instance, Esther was beset by anxiety, because she knows that writing publicly about these issues is risky.

I first met Grace at the South by Southwest Interactive Media Festival (SXSW) in Austin, Texas. She is a White investigative reporter in her 30s, and has recently started writing books. Years of digital abuse have left her feeling apprehensive, a wariness I could sense when I introduced myself. During our subsequent interview, she said to me: "I'm always preparing for the backlash, and sometimes there isn't one and it's like, 'Oh. Good. Good thing.'" When I asked Grace to elaborate about "preparing for the backlash," she told me she was mentally preparing, explaining: "It helps me to set an expectation that I will. . . . I think some of the hardest moments are when you get the backlash and you didn't expect that this [article or book] would lead to that." She prefers to stay en garde than to risk being blindsided.

Rina was one of many women attacked online in the periphery of the GamerGate harassment campaign. Although the attacks against her were far less dramatic than those experienced by the women at the center of the controversy, Rina feared the mob would resurface. She is an academic who studies video gaming and inequality and had become wary of visibility. In telling me about an academic paper that she wrote on gaming, she said,

> I wasn't nervous when I wrote it. I was nervous after it got accepted. As soon as the article dropped, like as soon as it was out there, I was just like, what's going to happen? I was constantly checking everything,

Twitter and everything else, to see what would happen. When it did finally go there [to online attacks], I was certainly not surprised.

Anti-feminist gamers, for Rina, were predictable. They would strike; she just didn't know when. And their threats weren't play, for her:

> I have a small child and I had a few moments where I realized I needed to go online and delete anything linking identifiers to where I live. It's very hard to do that. People are constantly publishing all that information, and so I had to sort of prepare myself for the possibility that I could get doxxed, and that was scary.

Publishing is essential for Rina, required for her career, and it had become nerve-wracking.

About three-quarters of the women I spoke with described their lives as punctuated by fear: fear about what *could* happen at any given moment, and for those whose abuse had subsided, fear that it would return. Scarlett is an introspective White game designer and academic in her 30s, with a talent for evocative descriptions that made me want to listen to her all day. She was pummeled by a firestorm of misogynistic abuse on YouTube and via email in response to an educational game she helped create that addressed a controversial issue. The attacks subsided by the time we spoke, but her fear remained. Rather than feeling as though the attack was difficult, but behind her, Scarlett experienced it as foreshadowing—a harbinger of worse to come.

> I felt physically exposed. I felt like it would be so easy for someone to find me, and nobody's trying to *not* let them find me. . . . I was just scared and so upset. I cannot imagine what it's like for people that are still having to live with this as part of their day-in, day-out life. For me, it's a thing that happened and it's a thing I'm aware will probably happen again, I don't know when. . . . Nothing happened [to the attackers]. . . . What does nothing mean when there's this constant electric current of fear running through everything in your professional life?

What a powerful formulation—the constant electric current of fear running through everything in her professional life. "Is that how you feel?," I asked. "Yes," she said. The psychological impact of digital harassment will be explored in Chapter 5, but for now suffice it to say that for women who have been attacked online, anticipatory fear is one way that the patterned resistance against them online becomes bigger than the sum of its parts.

IT'S PROBABLY FINE, RIGHT?

Uncertainty also contributes to the broad sense of uneasiness women feel in their digital lives. Unlike most other forms of harassment and violence women face, digital abuse from strangers usually comes with little information about the perpetrators. Even when attackers use their real names, there are precious few context cues available to help women assess the extent of the threat. Those attacked generally rarely know where the attackers are located, what they do for a living, whether they have a history of violence, or if they make a practice of being digitally abusive. They have no way of knowing whether the attacker is incensed and agitated, having a laugh, or has already moved on to something else. This uncertainty leaves victims second guessing themselves: Is this a big deal? Am I freaking out over nothing? Should I let someone know about this? Maybe I'm just being paranoid.

In the absence of body language or tone of voice, and with little context, women assess the risk of escalation with the limited information they have. In practice, this means measuring a given email, comment, or direct message against others they receive, comparing behaviors across attackers. In this context, attackers who are persistent and communiqués that appear to have required time and effort to create and send are particularly frightening. The women I interviewed interpreted their aggressors' labor as a testament to their determination and/or the depth of their hate. Annelise is a Black woman in her 30s whose accomplishments and breadth of experience belie her youthful appearance and demeanor. She has written several books on social justice issues and serves as the executive director of a nonprofit organization, a role that puts her in the national spotlight. She spoke of the investment of time as a red flag:

> When they make the effort, that's the thing that does stick with me, when people have gone through such effort to really, really create a nasty little meme or something like that. For example, when I went on CNN recently, they were talking about how [a political figure] had called these Black women [a racist nickname] in the workplace. Somebody tweeted at me a [meme based on her remarks] and then sent me an animated gif [graphics interchange format][on the same

theme]. I was thinking, "Wow, you took the time to actually go on an app and edit that and create [memes and gifs]"?

This sentiment was common. Billie, a White broadcaster and writer in her 40s, also circled back to the investment of time as disconcerting when we talked:

> I've had guys basically tell me they know where I go into my build-ing every day and they know what time I work and stuff like that. . . . There's a lot of photo shopping of my head onto like really fat women in pornographic positions, stuff like that. What bothers me is the fact that someone dislikes me so much they spent all this time creating this, that's really what bothers me . . . the fact that they went out of their way to do this. So, there's like a group of guys who have been after me for coming up on two years . . . telling me they hope I die, they hope I get raped, they hope someone kills me and rapes my body, and that stuff. . . . I've heard that stuff so many times now I'm just kind of like, "whatever," but the fact that they are so patient in doing it, and they are so dedicated to doing this to me every single day—that is really what disturbs me.

Several of the women in this study researched their aggressors, trying to put their behavior in context. In most cases, they knew the search was unlikely to put them at ease. Grace, for example, had been contacted by a convicted rapist on more than one occasion. He was upset about what she'd written about him. She reached out to other journalists working on the story to see whether they had been contacted; she thought if she learned he was lashing out at multiple journalists (rather than focused on her), she would feel better. It turned out her colleagues were being harassed, too. It did little to assuage her fears:

> This person has emailed many reporters because I went around to see if I could find other [journalists covering the story] and see what emails they got or whatever. But he lives here in the same state that I do, and he's not in prison anymore, or in jail. And he was very mad. And so I filed a police report because I understand how paper trails work, and I had said don't contact me again and he did so—that's enough, then you can file right? So it was one of those where I was like I don't think . . . my logical brain was that this is not gonna become anything, right? He didn't threaten me, he didn't insinuate that he

knows where I live. There was nothing there. But it was enough that I thought if something happened, I feel like I should have a paper trail. Just in case.

Although her "logical brain" wanted to believe she was safe, Grace feels unsafe enough that she decides to document the emails, in the event that she is physically victimized in the future. This is a window into the insecurity with which many women contend; The ambiguity surrounding the threats enhance the turmoil. Women have to manage credible threats, but they also become embroiled in exhausting exercises in risk assessment and self-doubt that compounds their sense of danger.

LONG ARMS

The same mobile technologies that give us the miraculous ability to communicate with our friends and family nearly anytime and anywhere also provide scaffolding for hostile speaking environments. These tools give online abuse and harassment unprecedented geographical and temporal reach. Violet, a straight-talking writer and social media manager who identifies racially as a Pacific Islander, has experienced episodic digital attacks. Recently, after a mild disagreement with someone on Twitter, the coordinated retaliation turned her phone into a weapon:

> It just felt, I don't know if it's Pavlovian, but every time I saw my phone, I would have anxiety. Because I knew that I needed to be online to do work, and to get messages from people I love, and check in with my kids. But I didn't want to even open it. I took all the notifications off my phone, because I would wake up in the morning to all these hate messages. . . . I had these dudes, it felt like they were just hammering me every day about how terrible I was. And over nothing, so it felt even stranger to me. Because I didn't feel like I was out there saying anything really that crazy. I wasn't rocking the boat, you know what I mean?

Mobile technologies mean that respite from digital harassment can feel even harder to find than respite from street harassment or sexual harassment in the workplace. In this respect, this form of abuse mirrors what researchers have learned about cyberbullying among young people: the hate is in your pocket (Patchin and Hinduja 2006; Slonje and Smith 2008). As Rina said, "I'll be sitting there with my phone, I'll be like, should I check? Then it feels like bricks." Many attackers follow women across platforms, and some gain access to their targets' personal contact information such as email addresses and phone numbers, making the toxicity feel inescapable.

Hazel, a woman in her mid-30s, was the subject of digital hate so profound and sustained that the attacks against her became national news. She described an experience she had walking out of a public lecture:

> I go give this wonderful speech and as soon as I leave, I look down at my phone and I get people saying things like, "I'm waiting outside your house for you to get back from [redacted]. Your dogs are going to die. The last thing you're ever going to feel is a drill bit going into your skull and seeing your husband murdered."

Hazel was disgusted and frightened by these kinds of attacks, but also righteously angry at their ability to infiltrate her life. It was hard for her to ever really feel free. Similarly, Aubrey found that technology had a way of enmeshing abuse in her day-to-day existence. She is a White, award-winning journalist and author in her 30s with nearly 80,000 followers on Twitter. She finds it impossible to get away. She told me to think about it: "Imagine trying to do your work or chat with someone online, but every time you do anything a pop-up window with porn comes up or something like violence or whatever, or just like expletives and stuff . . . " It's omnipresent.

The diffuse experiences—of anticipatory fear, of uncertainty and second-guessing, and of being confronted with hateful content when you least expect it—help illuminate why it is hard for outsiders to understand the experiences of those who navigate targeted attacks. This climate is more disorienting and omnipresent than a tally of threats, insults, or pornographic gifs can communicate.

Being a Woman in a Context of Contempt

As overwhelming as the digital speaking environment feels, gender-based attacks online are one component in a weighty tapestry of devaluation, discrimination, hostility, and violence familiar to most women. For some, these indignations are ameliorated by privileges of race, class, citizenship, and profession, but all the women I spoke with, even those most privileged, reflected on the costs of being a woman in a context of contempt, where men are often predatory. In fact, some spoke of the digital toxicity as particularly upsetting because it reminded them of the hostility toward women that exists in other public spaces. Aubrey addressed this explicitly:

> It's a reminder of this [general] climate of un-safety that we live in and that women are subjected to. [It's a reminder of the reality] that I can be raped and the odds of my rapist being even arrested— let alone convicted—are low. I mean, the odds of a rapist being con- victed is minuscule, and it's minuscule all over the world, and so most women go through their lives at least somewhat afraid of rape and we don't even, I think, most women don't even think about the fact that's not a reality shared by everyone. . . . Obviously men are raped and that's sad too, but on the whole I think the majority of men don't go through their normal lives in normal public space with [rape] as a fear . . . like that's what makes [digital] misogyny and sexism and whatever you want to call it so offensive—it's not just discrimination, it's a reminder that the world is not for us in a way.

Digital attacks are, then, part of a broader world contoured by the fear of male violence. Aubrey's account reminds us how accustomed women have become to following the rules of public space—to consulting their mental maps. Her fear of attack online called her attention to the how *normal* the fear and vigi- lance she exercises in physical spaces have become. This is what her life is like offline, too.

The women I interviewed made regular analogies to abuse in other public spaces as a way to help me better understand their experiences with digital hostility. At another point in our interview, Aubrey told me that it was hard to explain it all to an outsider. Initially, I though she meant that it upset her to discuss it, but she corrected me: it was literally hard to make someone else understand what the hate felt like. She used her experience with gender-based harassment offline as a way to tell her story:

> I mean, it's not so much like emotionally too hard for me to talk about, it's just that [it's hard to describe]. I don't really know . . . [pro- longed pause] I mean it reminds me, I had a stalker in my early 20s, and there's this thing where you just don't feel safe anywhere. Just

walking down the street, you feel like you have to be kind of on alert just in a way that . . . I spend most of my time in cities, and so I move through the world with a certain amount of awareness . . . but there's this different thing when you wonder "is somebody going to come after me?" I don't know, I know it's just . . . it is hard to describe. I don't know how. It's such an abstract feeling of intense stress, and you're just worried . . . it's just stressful to feel, to have the sense that many people who are strangers to you, who hate you for nothing that has to do with you as an individual, are taking pleasure in and putting a lot of energy into making your life bad and hurting you in different ways.

Digital abuse is delivered in new ways and has a different taxonomy of harms than other forms of violence against women, but this experience of gendered hostility and the pervasive sense of "un-safety" were not new to Aubrey. Many of the women who shared their accounts with me made connections among their experiences with gendered hostility on and offline.

CONTINUUM

Some women describe the attitudes toward them online as par for the course, in keeping with the subtle and not-so-subtle sexism and misogyny they deal with regularly. Jill, a White public intellectual, blogger, and academic in her 40s, said,

It's always gender and it's always sexualized, whether or not the thing they're mad about is about gender and sex. So, you know, nobody ever just calls me an asshole. They always call me a cunt or a bitch, right? Almost always, the violence is sexual. So, it's not like, "I want to punch you in the face." It's always, "I want punch you in the cunt." Right, always, always. . . . That's just being a woman in America. . . . My classroom is sexist. Like, what I look like can shape how people react to me in my classroom. The reception of my book is sexist; I lost a few pounds before I went on book tour because I didn't want people to be like, "I'm not gonna listen to some fat girl talk.". . . Right? Like I recognize I don't have the luxury of going on a book tour with extra pounds on me, right? But like, my dating life is sexist. My appearance is far more valued than a heterosexual man on the dating market. Like, there's nothing about [digital abuse] that is different from the sexism I experience, and have experienced, my whole life. . . . No new experience there.

And listen to Sophia:

> I mean, ["random" sexism is] just the craziest thing. I remember leaving a party one time, looking for a taxi, down in the East Village, and how the taxi driver . . . I mean, I was in a coat. I was leaving a party. A taxi driver started screaming at me that I was a whore, and I was like, what? It was just one of those . . . I just remember thinking like, that's, it's just the craziest things that can happen. In the course of a day, you have no idea what's gonna be screamed at you. I mean, that isn't the experience that my husband has, at all. So, that is just one of the realities that we deal with as women, and I'm not saying it's okay. But like, walking by a construction site, and you take a minute where you're like, ah, here we go. Or, you put on headphones, so you don't have to listen to it. So, I suppose being a woman and a reporter, is a little bit like that. Your male colleagues are, certainly, getting berated just as much, but the misogynistic, the gender-focused debasement is not present.

Stories like this one emerged repeatedly. Jill's frustration captures the continuity across venues, from her classroom to her book tour, dating, and digital life, and Sophia points to just a sampling of the various public spaces in which she has been made to feel uncomfortable.

Women also pointed toward the continuity of gender-based harassment over time. Alex, a White, well-established professor who loves to talk politics on Twitter, traced sexualized abuse throughout her lifetime. It's been an unwelcome constant since childhood:

> Ever since I was a kid, I was very much bullied by the boys on the school bus. . . . my bus ride to school was about 45 minutes long. And it was torture. It was probably the most torturous part of my entire childhood. I grew up in a working-class, blue-collar town, and there were a lot of boys who sat in the back of the bus. . . . For some reason, I also felt like I kind of wanted to sit in the back of the bus. I wasn't anything like them. I was a goody two-shoes, but I liked the excitement of "What goes on in the back of the bus?" And I paid the

price for that inclination. They were awful. They were awful. They asked me if I gave my trumpet a blow job. One of them, when I was in fourth grade, asked me if I washed my clit, and I didn't know what that was. And so I said, "No!" And then that was like, "Oh, she doesn't wash her clit." It was all sexual. . . . It was constant.

Casey, a White academic in her 50s, is a highly regarded expert who publishes and speaks about several male-dominated arenas including technology, sports, and gaming. Her attempts to manage the threat of digital harassment, she told me, mirrored the way she attempted to manage the threat of rape. To her, it was an apt analogy. Women navigating these spaces invest a lot of added mental and emotional labor, she said, voice heavy with resignation. "I think many of us are used to making all kinds of constant small calculations and so this is just another in the—it's very naturalized."

Acknowledging the Hostile Speaking Environment

Consistent efforts to shame, intimidate, and discredit women online combine to create a hostile speaking environment, analogous to the hostile work environment discussed in the context of employment discrimination. As we hear in my participants' accounts, digital attacks foster an unreasonably and inequitably abusive climate for women who enter. And although specific tweets, emails, and comments are disturbing, the true weight of online abuse emerges in its cumulative impact. The culture is so risk-prone and pervasively toxic that the hostility constrains women *even in its absence*, just as Carol Brooks Gardner (1995) described in her pioneering work on street harassment. The climate unsettles and antagonizes women such that writing and speaking in these contexts poses professional, social, physical, and emotional risks. Making matters worse, this precarity is only magnified by the way the sexualized attention and hostility women experience in these contexts corresponds to and heightens women's awareness of the misogyny they face in other public spaces, a steady reminder that they are only as valuable as they are sexually desirable.

While the conceptual framework of the hostile climate helps us understand the experiences of women online, it also raises a red flag: Hostile speaking environments lack the legal structures and avenues of recourse in place to address employment discrimination. It is crucial that women attacked online have recourse to address the hostile speaking environments they encounter. This is not to suggest that sexual harassment at work or online harassment are mutually exclusive. The structures in place to address workplace harassment must be adapted to acknowledge that when women work online, those digitals experiences become part of their workplace.

Regardless of whether digital harassment and toxicity are linked to the workplace, the next chapter shows that women dealing with digital abuse find it nearly impossible to hold attackers accountable. In the absence of laws that criminalize such public attacks, they are left to try to protect themselves or attempt to leverage laws intended for other purposes (usually with minimal success). Their abusers, those engaging in digital misogyny and racism, have a distinct advantage: the ability to wreak havoc, to build and maintain a speaking environment that is truly hostile, with impunity.

2

Just Get Off the Internet

As destructive as the abuse can be, women's experiences with online attacks are frequently trivialized—structurally and culturally. On the structural side, both the US legal system and the social media platforms where the majority of the abuse transpires fail women as their attacker and attack-focused accountability systems are incapable of addressing the cumulative phenomena. Meanwhile, cultural beliefs that privilege physical over nonphysical harm, construct digital harassment as the victim's fault, and maintain a false dichotomy between digital and "real" life trivialize the problem. The trivialization is so pervasive that victims have internalized it: they minimize their own experiences, even as they vociferously resist others' attempts to do so. They find themselves in a double-bind: aware of the culture and structures that minimize their experiences and struggling with their own internalized trivialization, the women I interviewed rarely reported their abuse. When they did report, it was seldom gratifying. In the face of the commonly held and normalizing assumption that hateful abuse is part and parcel of life online, targets are left with the perception that the onus is on them to get out of harm's way.

Tree Solutions to Forest Problems

At first blush, it appears as though opportunities for recourse are plentiful. In the United States, where most of the respondents for this study are based, there are many potential pathways for legal action. These range from criminal penalties for stalking, harassment, or threats of violence to tort claims for infractions such as defamation and intentional infliction of emotional distress. To the extent that online harassment threatens to drive people from protected groups offline, civil rights laws, designed to punish abuse motivated by race,

Credible Threat. Sarah Sobieraj, Oxford University Press (2020). © Oxford University Press.
DOI: 10.1093/oso/9780190089283.001.0001.

national origin, religion, and (in some states) gender and sexual orientation, open another possible path of ameliorative action (Citron 2014).

However, US law is centered around suspects and their individual actions, and these options are ill-equipped to address the harm caused by many forms of digital abuse. For most of the women in this research, the impact of identity-based abuse comes not from navigating one-off abusive communiqués or even persistent harassers (although several of the women also dealt with a persistent harasser or stalker) but from coping with a deluge of poison-tipped darts, thrown by many different people, across multiple platforms in crescendos and decrescendos over time.

When the cumulative abuse is dismantled into its constituent parts, most individual attacks fall short of the threshold for legal action. This came up repeatedly as my participants talked about seeking legal remedies. Annelise, the Black nonprofit executive, coped with repeated death and rape threats, some of which were overtly gendered and radicalized. And although she was reflective and self-possessed as she described these experiences, Annelise lapsed into exasperation when she explained why she rarely reports the threats that she receives to the police:

> I got a combination rape and death threat, and they also simultaneously harassed my husband and threatened him to get to me after I appeared on [a conservative TV program]. That was kind of one of those days where [the threats and harassment] got to me, and it made me really angry. And it wasn't even so much that the content of it was scary—to have someone threaten your life and describe in great detail how they would rape you and how they would kill you—it was also the fact that law enforcement's response to it was so problematic. . . . They came by my apartment and just basically said, "Well, there's nothing we can do because this person used the conditional tense" and "They kind of know what they're doing." And "They kind of need to be more clear about when they would kill you, when they would rape you, and where, for us to do this. So, there's not much we can do, but keep us posted if anything else happens."

Parsing verb tense matters for the officers because they need to determine whether they have a crime on their hands, but it is insulting and perplexing for a frightened victim. Kimberly, a young, White writer at a major newspaper, has faced less digital abuse than others in this study, but her bad experiences were still upsetting. Reminiscent of Annelise, Kimberly felt as upset by the police response as she was by the first serious threats that came her way:

> A couple days later, I got this really violent, threatening email basically saying like . . . They said something about me being lesbian and "you need to be taken to such and such place and gang-raped continuously" for X-amount of time. . . . They [the local police] told me, "There's nothing we can really do, but if there's ever any kind of hate crime or something that happens in the area, this guy will be on a short list." Which was just really dissatisfying. . . . Like, I really wanted to [ask] them, "Really, that's it? You're going to wait for him to do something completely terrible before you arrest him?"

It is a crime to threaten someone with physical harm if the threat is *credible*— if the target might reasonably believe the threat is serious, could feasibly be carried out, and that the danger is imminent. These criteria are intended to weed out hypothetical comments made without serious intent, such as friends saying, "I'm going to kill you" in jest. Yet in practice, these criteria mean that for a threat to be criminal, it must specify exactly how the sender intends to inflict harm, the authorities need to believe that the person making the threat might reasonably be able to follow through with these plans, and that they could do so at any moment.

Debbie, the sardonic pundit who heads a nonprofit advocacy group, once had an FBI agent tell her that a threat was not actionable because the violence described was to be meted out with a hairbrush. The FBI agent thought it was unrealistic. The policies are well-intended, but come with a host of collateral consequences. Many attackers are savvy, knowing enough to tailor their harassment so that it falls within the bounds of the law while still being very disturbing. In the context of the victims' experiences, in which a specific threat being reviewed by law enforcement is often just one of many unsettling messages, emails, comments, or tweets, this threshold for action compounds women's anxiety and anger by making them feel powerlessness.

The same obstacle affects people attempting to use tort law to deal with online harassment. Maya is a Black activist and writer in her 30s. She is sharp, sophisticated, and noticeably guarded. Maya was upset when someone posted outrageous misinformation about her online. She worried that it would affect her reputation and ability to find work, so she pursued a civil suit for defamation. Maya wanted the record corrected. But because Maya had appeared on television and in a documentary speaking about a gender justice issue, legal avenues were closed to her: "When people write defamatory things about me," Maya explained, "attorneys have told me that I can't sue [successfully] because I'm a public figure . . . because she [the attorney] has to prove actual malice."

Maya, like many women who are vocal about social or political issues, can be legally classified as a "limited-purpose public figure." The term refers to "one who voluntarily becomes a key figure in a particular controversy, or one who has gained prominence in a particular, limited field, but whose celebrity has not reached an all-encompassing level" ("Proving Fault: Actual Malice and Negligence" n.d.). And when the plaintiff in a defamation case is considered a public figure, the person's legal team must establish that the information was published with "actual malice," showing that the defendant "knew that the statement was false or acted with reckless disregard to the truth of the statement."[1] That is, the publisher's state of mind at the time of publication is a determining factor in establishing malice. This means the burden of proof is heavier for public figures, a policy intended to foster open debate about important issues without fear of litigation ("Proving Fault: Actual Malice and Negligence" n.d.). It is a virtuous intention, but the effect is frequently harmful. For Maya, this was upsetting, not because this particular attacker had been the primary source of the harassment leveled against her, but because the collective harassment in response to her advocacy was overwhelming, and she believed that at least this *particular* behavior would be within the reach of the law. She sought legal action because she needed to draw a line somewhere; the legal system was unable to draw that line for her.

These legal thresholds prevent Annelise, Kimberly, Debbie, and Maya from being able to use the law to hold many of their attackers accountable, and, by extension, from deterring others who might be potential abusers. But lowering the threshold is not the solution. Victim-initiated legal pursuit of individual perpetrators is not a robust approach to digital attacks in which targets are being hounded by dozens of people in myriad ways across multiple platforms. What's more, attacker-centered accountability only works when you can identify your harassers. This is impossible when attackers use anonymity to their advantage, posting on platforms that do not collect IP (internet protocol) addresses or taking precautions such as sending hateful content from public computers in libraries, universities, office supply stores, and hotel business centers. Ivy, a young, White expert on tech culture at a high profile national newspaper, wanted to get a restraining order against a persistent harasser, but that meant establishing a pattern of sustained harassment. This proved an almost insurmountable challenge: Ivy's attacker used technologies that made his identity hard to detect, created multiple accounts to make it look as though the abuse was coming from different people, and worked across multiple platforms:

> In order to prove that he had done this on three occasions, we had to show that these [different] online profiles that he was using to comment on the newspaper's site were all coming from him, even though they were under false names. We had to show that they were from the same IP address. Threats that he was making on Twitter, I knew it was him, but I couldn't prove it, because the police wouldn't investigate, so those weren't a part of it. . . . He had this thing that originates a different IP address for you. In one case, he had slipped up and done one of these anonymous threats under the same IP address that he had commented under his actual name like at the same time. . . . He had sent emails to me and my boss. . . . He did these anonymous comments on the site, many more than we could actually prove were from him. He called me, and then he started these Twitter accounts. Those I couldn't prove at all, because Twitter won't tell you anything. . . . In a way, I feel like all harassing trolls kind of sound the same, like they talk the same, and so that's confusing because I don't know if it's him or not, and I suspect that some of them are him. I feel like the police should take it more seriously because he needs to stop doing this. . . . But because it's on Twitter, the police won't do anything and Twitter won't do anything and I can't even figure out who it is. I don't know how scared of him I should be.

After meeting with her employer, investigating on her own time, working with attorneys, and appearing in court—in the same room with the stalker—repeatedly, Ivy eventually obtained the restraining order. Still, her success hinged on an unlikely convergence of facts: the perpetrator lashed out at her via the comment section of the newspaper where she worked, her employer gave her access to user data from the inward-facing side of the newspaper, and the otherwise careful harasser made a mistake as he tried to obscure his identity. What's more, Ivy had the resources necessary to invest in this endeavor. Had the perpetrator limited his abuse to one outlet (say, Twitter or YouTube or Facebook) or had her employer been unwilling to share user data from their website, she could not have proven that the attacks were coming from the same person.

Listening to the women I interviewed, it becomes clear that addressing digital harassment via the legal system is frustrating. In many cases, women find a lack of meaningful actions available, and those who are able to use the law to hold a particular harasser accountable find the attacker-by-attacker strategy more time consuming than fruitful, given the emotional and logistical realities of collective (and often anonymized) harassment.

Many more women seek support from the platforms on which their identity-based attacks take place, something that seems promising at first blush. Virtually all online news outlets that allow commenting have community guidelines in place that prohibit harassment, ad hominem attacks, and the use of derogatory language. Many news organizations have in-house moderation. Prominent social media platforms such as Twitter, Facebook, Instagram, and YouTube all have terms of service that explicitly reject digital abuse.

Given its reputation for ugliness, it may surprise some to learn that abuse and harassment are prohibited on Twitter. As the Twitter Rules state, "You may not engage in the targeted harassment of someone, or incite other people to do so. This includes wishing or hoping that someone experiences physical harm." "Hateful Conduct" is also forbidden by Twitter: "You may not promote violence against, threaten, or harass other people on the basis of race, ethnicity, national origin, sexual orientation, gender, gender identity, religious affiliation, age, disability, or serious disease" ("The Twitter Rules" n.d.). But such prohibitions are ineffective without meaningful enforcement. And violations rarely come with meaningful consequences; the outcome are policies that function as guidelines.

This is not to say that social media platforms are indifferent to enforcement. Facebook, for example, uses artificial intelligence, community flagging features, and 15,000 global content reviewers (counting full- and part-time employees, as well as those working via third-party contractors), a number that has tripled since 2017 (Madrigal 2018; Wong 2019). Twitter reportedly took action against nearly 300,000 user accounts in the first six months of 2018 (Chen 2019). That responsiveness is promising, although less impressive when we consider that there are approximately 330 *million* active Twitter accounts at the time of this writing. In spite of these policies and the efforts to enforce them, the women I spoke with have mixed feelings about their preferred social media platforms' commitment to fighting abuse.

Many respondents take advantage of feed filtering tools, opting to mute, block, and/or hide comments and direct messages from those who are hostile. For some, these options are vital tools to help manage digital life. Lynette, the Black public intellectual, said it took her a while to stop worrying about upsetting people by blocking them, but now she sees it as an indispensable tool: "I do it with impunity. I don't need any reason to block you anymore. . . . That's actually one of the first things I suggest to people when I reach out to them [about digital abuse]. 'Get over that fast, block everybody you need to block.'" Grace, the investigative journalist I met at SXSW, is a fan of muting: "For all the hate that Twitter gets, being able to mute conversations, mute in general, is a great feature." She uses muting and hiding users in lieu of reporting abusive content to the platform. It's a relatively low-key way to reduce the hostility she faces: "These very small things," she said, "like being able to post something on Facebook and then being able to turn off notifications on that post and just never see people's responses—that's fine."

Other women feared that icing-out their attackers would prompt them to escalate their abuse via other channels. This is not an unfounded fear: abusive critics who have been blocked sometimes post the block notice on a discussion board or on their own social media accounts, encouraging others to retaliate. Worried about backlash, Scarlett, the game designer, follows Grace's method by muting and hiding rather than blocking, because harassers remain unaware of muting and hiding but are usually able to find out about the blocking.

Filtering tools are appreciated, but few feel they stop abusers. I met Naomi, a White undergraduate computer science major, when she was on the brink of graduation. We met after both attending the same public lecture about digital harassment in gaming. Naomi recalled that her experience of identity-based vitriol started when she was in middle school and participating on anonymous chat sites like Omegle and in role-playing games. As an outspoken queer Jewish woman, Naomi has always found digital communities important, and the value of these niches only intensified as she began to enter more male-dominated spaces offline. She continues to appreciate social media for providing her with spaces to address social issues, particularly LGBTQ issues, but finds they are periodically punctuated with almost unbearable abuse. She told me about an anti-Semitic threat, for example, that described raping her in a gas chamber and included a chilling description of wolves ripping off her limbs. Naomi is open to blocking attackers so that they cannot ruin the spaces she values, but remains frustrated that the people she blocks face no consequences, especially on her favorite platform, Tumblr:

My personal response has been to block or ignore or if [the platform] has a simple option to flag the user for harassment or something, but for anonymous Tumblrs your options are either to respond or block. There is no way to report the anonymous user, so when people have usernames—like the YouTube comments or something—I'll generally flag or report it, but the problem with Tumblr is that there is no way to really track them. It's just block. There is no repercussion.

The lack of meaningful alternatives is something Naomi raised repeatedly while we spoke. She started to cry when she told me about seeing her best friend attacked, feeling at least as upset with Tumblr as with the attackers themselves, because flagging and reporting do not do enough:

My best friend—I remember when her dog died. I know what her favorite soup is. She didn't publish all of them, but she published some of these like horrible comments—It makes me very upset [wells up]—these horribly graphic, harassment things [crying]. It's like, I know [struggles to talk] Sorry. I know how good of a person she is and she's someone who I want to protect because, you know, she's my best friend. . . . As a computer science major, I've put in google analytics and tried to find as many ways as I can to track people if they try to harass me, but if you're not tech savvy—even if you are tech savvy—there's so little put in place! My biggest criticism of Tumblr is infrastructure. There is very little to nothing put in place to save you from these people. It's that helpless feeling of not being able to help them. I think that's also a big distinction between the internet and in person, because if someone were to come up to me and my best friend on the street, I would knock their lights out because I'm a third degree black belt! But when someone does it on the Internet, there's nothing I can do to help them and protect them.

A few of the women I spoke with were actively opposed to using filtering tools. Willa is a sharp, charismatic White woman in her 20s with a freshly minted PhD who works in the technology sector. She was targeted by a swift, menacing attack coordinated on 4chan after she participated in anti-racism discourse on Twitter. During the attack, hackers took over her most visible social media account and began posting offensive content in her name, hoping to discredit her and damage her career. Willa waded through death and rape threats, gender-based abuse, and unsettling pornographic images. Still, she felt strongly that if content of that nature was out there, directed at her, she needed to know. "If I blocked these people, especially while things are still happening, then I wouldn't see anything else that they send me, right?" Willa paused pointedly to let me to connect the dots. Obscuring those voices—especially the most hateful—felt too risky. She continued:

> It's not doing anything to discourage the underlying behavior, and for me, it's really just like this ignorance is bliss mentality. "Oh, they're not in my @mentions, so it's not affecting me." When, in reality, if everyone else on Twitter can see those awful tweets and I'm just not seeing it, I feel like that puts me at a disadvantage, more than anything.

Willa resents the way the tools seem to turn victims into moderators: "I'm very opposed to muting and blocking as a strategy for dealing with abuse. I feel like it's more work for the victim. The person suffering abuse is now tasked with muting and blocking all of these accounts." This sentiment was widely shared across my sample—the time it takes to filter and report abusive content—is costly, as I explore more fully in Chapter 5.

In contrast to the complex reactions to feed filtering tools, most participants supported flagging and reporting abusive content and accounts. Alex, the professor, was easily the most enthusiastic. Alex is a prolific Twitter user and sees using the platform as an extension of her academic life. She regularly posts about American politics, offering expert explainers on American democracy, issuing calls for political reform, and political snark with entertaining anecdotes from her personal and professional life thrown in for good measure. She had low-expectations when it came to Twitter's commitment to supporting a healthy climate, since she received gender-based, acrimonious feedback often, but Alex was impressed by how well Twitter's tools worked:

> The way that I did start to reclaim some agency, actually, was I started just muting people and then reporting them. And that felt really good. I even had a few Twitter accounts that were temporarily suspended, which surprised me. I actually didn't expect any recourse from Twitter. I just wanted to report people to make myself feel like I was doing something. I had heard that Twitter is not particularly good about taking action . . . so when I did report, and then a day

later, I got an e-mail that that particular user's account had been suspended, I was like, "No way!" That felt amazing. Right? Because you also know . . . they don't know you did it—I'm sure I'm not the only person that they're calling a bitch or a cunt. It could be anyone that they have offended or attacked could have reported them. So that felt really good.

Grace, too, has seen some response in the rare cases she chose to lodge a formal complaint: "I so rarely report abuse. . . . But maybe that's because I don't believe that anything will happen if I do. I did report someone recently and Twitter shut down their account. I had to report someone to Goodreads, and Goodreads shut that down." In pressing her about why she feels pessimistic, given these minor successes, she made it clear that the problem is too big to be solved this way. Grace is attacked via email, on Twitter, on Facebook, and in the comment sections that follow her articles. Reporting someone might make that particular account disappear, like a wet footprint drying on tile by the side of a pool, but for Grace, the pool is crowded and chaotic. New prints are constantly in the making.

It is important that platforms provide features such as filtering tools and pathways to flag and report content—indeed, many of these features have been introduced at the urging of advocates and nongovernmental organizations (NGOs) advocating on behalf of abuse victims—but like existing criminal and civil legal structures, these innovations are ill-equipped to truly address the cumulative experience of operating in a hostile speaking environment.

It's Just People Online: Trivializing Narratives

"You are all a bunch of crybabies!" A number of years ago, at the outset of this research, I was on a public panel addressing the issue of anonymity and hostile behavior online. I was seated alongside a White journalist with experience in comment moderation and an Asian American man with minor celebrity status who had been the subject of digital abuse. When the moderator opened the floor for questions, a disheveled White man, probably in his mid-60s, approached the microphone. Rather than ask a question, he scoffed, "You are all a bunch of crybabies!" He then rolled his eyes, adopted a derisive boo-hoo voice, and lamented that people today can't handle it if someone "hurts their feelings." The commenter went on to offer some reprimands about people needing to develop a thick skin and a variant of "if you can't stand the heat, get out of the kitchen," before stepping away from the mic.

This response felt surprising at the time, but as my research unfolded, I realized his interpretation of online harassment was common. People make a number of assumptions that result in trivializing the kinds of abuse that troubled my respondents. These assumptions include the notion that digital life and "real" life are somehow distinct, that nonphysical harms are insignificant and readily ignored, and that these attacks are easily avoided by being appropriately cautious when online. These resilient beliefs combine with the normalizing and victim-blaming assumption that this kind of harassment is an inevitable byproduct of life online, quickly remedied by "getting off the internet" (remaining silent). This culture of trivialization makes it difficult to speak out about digital abuse, build support for reforms, or stand up for the right to participate and be heard.

That night at the panel, I inadvertently helped to circulate one of these damaging narratives. Having worked with women targeted by online abuse, the commenter's dismissiveness put me on the defensive. I responded sharply, determined to make him take this issue seriously. These are not simply people with hurt feelings, I insisted, and described a woman who had been forced to leave her home to stay safe, another who needed to be accompanied by bomb-sniffing dogs. Yet, by insisting that the threat of violence should make this matter, I implied that other harms—those that are emotional, professional, social, and psychological—somehow fail to merit attention. My co-panelist who, unlike me, had himself been attacked, responded very differently. Refusing to let the questioner shame him, he offered a direct challenge, saying, "It *did* hurt my feelings . . . " before going on to talk in-depth about why the persistent toxicity mattered, even if it was—in the eyes of the commenter—"just" bullying.

PHYSICAL HARM AS THE ONLY REAL HARM

As we just saw, Annelise and Kimberly were unable to obtain police support in the absence of a physical attack or what authorities believed was a "credible" threat of physical harm. Legally, Annelise and Kimberly's fear and sense of danger were irrelevant. Major social media platforms are similarly most responsive when threats of physical harm are at play. The potential for non-physical harm is taken far less seriously, with the exception of established

courses of behavior by a persistent harasser. Police and platform deprioriti-
zation of nonphysical harms aligns with the cultural narratives about what
counts as concern-worthy digital behavior. Billie encountered this thinking
when she approached her employer about the toll constant harassment was
taking on her life. The television network, she told me, "doesn't do anything"
about the high volume of body-commentary, gender-based insults, epithets,
and threats she receives. "They don't care, I've had meetings with HR and with
my boss and they've basically been like, 'Beyond physical safety, I don't know
what you want us to do.' So it's that. It's the refusal to acknowledge that this is
so much harder for me."

The constant humiliation and cruelty matter to her, as they would to most
people. But her employer treats these outcomes as beyond the network's pur-
view, even though Billie is targeted in direct response to the work she does for
the network and the abuse often comes via her network-linked social media
accounts and email. She felt Twitter dismissed the nonphysical harms as well:

> There's a reason we don't let people just follow people around and
> scream at them on the street, it's because it's horrible for the victim
> that it's happening to and this is exactly the same, only there are
> absolutely no repercussions for these people. . . . [P]eople are out
> there trying to ruin my reputation and the only thing I have, the only
> recourse I have is Twitter saying "Oh, well this doesn't violate our
> community guidelines because they're not threatening to kill you, so
> there's just nothing we can do." There's absolutely zero recourse. . . .
> It's beyond frustrating, and no one should have to live like this.

Throughout the interviews for this book, I also heard women whose
friends, family, and peers brushed aside their experiences. After Hazel's digital
abuse was in the news, people in her life wanted to talk with her about it, but
several failed to understand why the abuse was traumatic for her.

> By minimizing what I've gone through or by treating it [the abuse]
> like just another pop culture thing they have an opinion on . . . it hurts
> me. I come to tears every time I talk about it. I find a lot of men in
> my life . . . have no understanding of just how difficult that is. I think
> people are dismissive of it—I think they don't understand the silenc-
> ing effect.

No one in this study was physically assaulted by someone who threatened them online, but virtually all had been harmed. Many continue to bear weighty burdens, explored more fully in Chapter 5. For now, suffice it to say that failing to take nonphysical harm seriously does a disservice to victims. Diana is a 30-year-old businesswoman of Asian descent who survived vicious identity-based attacks while she was a blogger and columnist. She struggled with a cyberstalker who haunted her life for nearly a decade. In taking stock, Diana shook her head, commenting, "I've come to this position that trauma is trauma. Trauma isn't [only] something that happens to your body, and I think that's what most people misunderstand."

THE REAL WORLD

Sociologist Nathan Jurgenson coined the term "digital dualism" to describe the false sense that digital and "real" life are distinct, separate spheres (Jurgenson 2012; 2011). Digital dualism is a false binary because our online lives and our offline lives are inextricably linked. Jurgenson (2011) writes,

> What research as well as those who actually use social media tell us is that social media has everything to do with the physical world and our offline lives are increasingly influenced by social media, even when logged off. We need to shed the digital dualist bias because our Facebook pages are indeed "real life" and our offline existence is increasingly virtual.

The women in my study constantly brushed up against digital dualism as those around them suggested their experiences on online were somehow bracketed off from the feelings, experiences, and ideas we have when we disconnect. Anastasia is a Black journalist and blogger in her 40s, with a great sense of humor and a penchant for swearing. She addressed this fallacy directly:

> This idea that online life is different than offline life, is hilarious to me. Because, again, you're suffering the same humiliations, the same microaggressions and macroaggressions, on and offline. The shit isn't different. For folks to say . . . it's just Twitter. No, motherfucker, it's real life. And it happens whenever I log off, whenever I walk outside. You can't separate the two. So, it's really insulting when people say that.

Anastasia describes the experiences she has online as part of a continuum of mistreatment (for more on the continuum, see Chapter 1) in order to highlight the flawed distinction between virtual and physical life and point out the illegitimacy of minimizing digital hostility. The way online abuse is dismissed also came up in my conversation with Lynette, when she described others' misconceptions about online attacks:

> The most common one—someone did this to a friend in an online group recently—she was scared to give a public talk, she's an author. She was scared to go to the talk, because someone had been stalking her online for quite some time and she knew that where she was giving the talk was in the same city where that person lived. People's immediate response in the group was, "Oh, yeah, it's horrible. I wouldn't worry about it, it's just something on the internet." I went, "Oh, no, no, no. Don't say that to her, first of all. Don't dismiss how afraid she is. She absolutely should be afraid, and we should be telling her how she can deal and live with this fear. Not that it's irrational or that she's crazy."

Rina, the academic gaming expert, told me about a time she was frustrated by a male peer who invoked the "it's just the internet" line of thinking:

> I was talking to him about what was going on, and he was like, "But I don't understand. These are just people online." Like, he clearly didn't get it. I said, "Well, first of all, it doesn't *stay* online. If you're doxxed, that affects your real life." Also, it's such a privileged position to be able to say, "Oh well, having somebody insult you online, just ignore it. It's just people online." I feel like if you haven't been insulted like that online, you don't know what that feels like. You just can't imagine how exhausting it is.

At times the police used this same working theory. Maya called the police after receiving a violent and sexually explicit image-based rape threat on Facebook. The first thing the detective told her was, "Well, we handle real crime, not internet crime." Lynnette, Rina, and Maya shared these stories in the context of their aggravation with circulating misunderstandings about digital abuse. Yet, in each account, the elephant in the room is the way these misperceptions are turned against women who want their harassment to be taken seriously.

VICTIM-BLAMING

In talking about this research, I find that most people can imagine what it would feel like to have a torrent of strangers flood your inbox, direct messages, comment sections, and @mentions with humiliating, frightening, and professionally stigmatizing content. We understand why being photoshopped into violent or pornographic scenes, receiving rape and death threats, being called a "cum dumpster" or "yellow skank," and/or having our "fuckability" debated in public—in full view of our colleagues, family, and community—might undermine our reputation, riddle us with anxiety, make us want to hole up, or distract us from our work. We think it is horrible that this happens and shake our heads in disgust. But most people sympathize at arm's length, in the same way they might feel badly when we learn a friend-of-a-friend has died unexpectedly. In both cases, people want to know the circumstances surrounding the tragedy. This desire is driven by concern and curiosity, but also by an implicit need to reassure ourselves that we are not in danger, because we do not smoke or drive under the influence.

In this regard, victim-blaming is not *just* about stereotypes, it is also about finding an explanation for horrible phenomena that allows us to imagine that we have control over our own safety. If the victim died, was raped, or was harassed online because of something she did, we reason that we can avoid her fate by getting mammograms, staying out of fraternity houses, or not talking about abortion on Twitter. There is security in these beliefs, but it is false. What's more, these myths are damaging. If we accept narratives centering victims' personal choice and control, we free platforms, employers, police, and even abusers from responsibility by suggesting that more scrupulous personal conduct is the solution. Annelise was horrified to hear such arguments from her own family:

> Even my father will say things like, "Well, you chose this lifestyle. You chose to be doing this work. You chose to be vocal. This is what's the result." I think a lot of it comes back to all the same issues like the irony, like the patriarchy, it's sexism, right? . . . It was not what I wanted to hear at all. It took the onus from the people who are actually impeding the freedom of other people. So that, I think, is a big

part of culture. I think it's a big part of culture that a man would feel like it's even okay to say to me, "Well, you chose this, because you're not behaving in the way that society tells you to."... [P]eople are like, "Oh, you're courting it if you are out in public. You need visibility, you're doing it for that. If you want to avoid this sort of thing, then you should keep to yourself and be quiet."

This response feels predictable in light of the parallels to discourses around rape and sexual harassment, but that does little to ameliorate its deleterious effects.

Alex's husband had a similar, if less accusatory, response when he found out men were lashing out at her, calling her a bitch and a cunt on Twitter. Though Alex sees online participation as part of her role as a scholar, her partner seemed to imply she should just log off:

My husband noticed that it bothered me. It bothered my husband a ton! A ton. . . . I would talk about it, and he was like, "Why do you put yourself in that position?" It's funny, because it's kind of victim-blaming, right? He wasn't saying it nasty, but he was like, "Why do you put yourself in positions where that is going to happen? Get out of there!" Basically just, "Stop! Stop! Don't!"

Lynette encounters this line of thinking constantly. She pointed out that while people don't explicitly say she should avoid the internet, she gets the message nonetheless. "They say it a little nicer so, 'Oh, gosh. If I were you . . .' I usually get it more like that. 'If I were you X, Y, and Z.'" The fact that this suggestion was couched in concern did not make it any less frustrating. To Lynette, their "solution" is not only misguided, it is destructive:

I get the motivation for saying it, but I also think a lot of people do not understand the realities of how we live and work right now. That's like telling someone, "Oh, if you're addicted to something on the internet, you should just get rid of the internet. You know what the internet does now, we know what that facilitates," right? It would be saying don't participate in this really important arena of life . . . that's not as viable an option for everybody. . . . I don't think that there's any version of my life or my career that happens as wonderfully as it has happened had I not been writing publicly and had I not been visible. There's no other way. If you think there is another way, that's probably because you've had the privilege of thinking there's another way. I just didn't have that. Where was I going to get all of this professionalization and professional networking? Where was that going to happen? Where was I going to stake some claim over my intellectual ideas? Who was going to give me permission for that?

Likewise, Hazel says that avoiding social media would derail her career:

> You can't get off Twitter, because that's how you get jobs now. Like, this is just a fact. I mean, the way you rise to prominence, the way you get conference invites or get well known in your field or just make friends [in your field] is through Twitter and Facebook.

The absurdity was not lost on the other women in the study. Like Lynette and Hazel, women routinely discussed how upsetting it was to have others insist they either accept the consequences of online participation or log off. They felt they needed to constantly remind others that they could ill afford to lose the voice, visibility, connections, and community afforded by digital life. While it might be technically possible, leaving social media platforms it is not a realistic approach to modern life, especially for those whose voices are so often silenced in other, overlapping ways. It would not work for Hazel, who struggles from the margins in an overwhelmingly male-dominated arena, or for Lynette, who as a woman of color in a White, male profession, could not thrive without finding mentors, community, and places to write other than those traditionally upheld by her department and discipline. And for politicians, journalists, activists, and others whose professional lives are predicated on visibility and public engagement, there are no functionally equivalent paths.

In many ways this is beside the point. Even if a target were to "opt" out of digital life, there are no guarantees that she would be safe from digital attacks. As with victim-blaming in the sexual assault context, there are no rules of internet behavior that can fully insulate you from risk. Many women have been targeted by hostile, humiliating treatment and defamation on discussion boards and social media platforms even when they do not participate personally (Citron 2009; 2014; Franks 2017; MacAllister 2016; Massanari 2017; Filipovic 2007). Avoiding "risky" behaviors, such as sharing views on political and social issues publicly, writing about controversial topics, and steering clear of notoriously abuse-laden platforms is not enough to stay out of the line of fire any more than wearing modest clothing or avoiding "bad" parts of town can ensure that you are not sexually assaulted. This must be repeated: being vocal online does not always trigger abuse, nor will logging off necessarily prevent it.

Internalized Trivialization

These trivializing narratives, legal criteria for action, and platform policies impact victims. The cultural and structural responses to their abuse live in the minds of the women I interviewed, shaping the way they frame their own experiences. My participants are infuriated when others minimize their abuse. Even so, respondent after respondent shared moments of palpable fear or visceral humiliation in one breath, only to minimize those very experiences in the next. The contours of the interviewees' self-scrutiny are familiar, linked directly to the way attacks are evaluated on a case-by-case basis, narratives that dismiss nonphysical harm, and the people in their circles who suggest abuse is inevitable. Those targeted come to use similar yardsticks to gauge their own feelings, as if they need permission to be upset. Stepping back, it becomes clear that the majority of women's digital abuse is written off as insignificant, and the big picture—the hostile speaking environment that inflicts such turmoil—becomes obscured, even to the women drowning in it.

Lucy is a White freelance science and technology journalist, who has published in many high-profile national and international venues. She has dealt with a steady drumbeat of "low-level," gender-based abuse (particularly commentary on her physical appearance), along with explicit images, pornographic gifs, and periodic rape and death threats. She is in her early 30s and on the upswing of an impressive career, but Lucy is already worn out. She and her co-workers navigate tedious misogyny, day in and day out. During our interview, when she described her experiences with digital abuse, Lucy was taken aback by how terrible it all sounded laid out in front of her, as if she were realizing it for the first time. This fresh perspective made her contemplate why she had not seen it earlier and why she so rarely reports the attacks to her employer or the police. Initially, Lucy suggested that downplaying the severity of the abuse was a way of coping. Upon further reflection, Lucy noticed that professional socialization played an important role:

Each individual thing you could probably brush off quite easily. Or at least, "Oh, okay, something has happened, but I can move on." But because it does just keep happening, it ticks away at you. You sort of . . . I don't know, I think you have to come up with a coping strategy for it. If you were to be horrified every time you receive something, that would happen the whole time. You kind of have to . . . I don't know, yeah. Maybe it ties also into being told initially to not feed the trolls.

Earlier in our interview, Lucy had told me, "I have always been taught, 'Don't feed the trolls, don't feed the trolls, don't respond. You are just giving them what they want.' Yet, on a weekly and daily basis, I'm receiving these things. . . . [I]t has become so frequent and so normal." Now she continued:

That was the thing that I was always told. You kind of started doing that, thinking that was the right thing to do and good advice. Then that probably helped normalize it, and then you don't stop to think about the individual things being said and how horrible they are.

In a later moment, Lucy seemed to suggest that she had re-decided that her abuse was not so serious after all, offering:

For me, humor is the better way to deal with it. I think almost an earnest rage—that is the thing that the trolls, that is the impact that they want to have. For me it feels better to dampen the blows, to take the piss out of it rather than to hold it up as a real threat. Although, I do think some people, when there are credible threats out there, I think those should be dealt with in a different way.

It is not insignificant that Lucy uses the legal standard to separate serious abuse from the abuse that should be laughed off. Although she is no stranger to threats herself, she sees only the "credible" ones as those to be taken seriously. Parker, who was the victim of a coordinated attack in response to her work on an erotic magazine, also used this language in assessing how to respond to the abuse:

I do remember looking into the police option . . . and wondering if I should ask the school for protection, but I don't think I did because

I don't think there was ever an actual credible threat made against me. I think if someone had posted "we're going to wait outside Parker's class and try to [murder her] tomorrow," I probably would have done something. But, "she is a slut"? I mean, you could argue that that's libel, and it is. I'm actually glad I didn't pursue it, because from what I understand, most people who do try to pursue a lawsuit or a prosecution or anything like that, they usually come up with nothing. It's usually laughed out of court . . . from what I understand.

Hundreds of pages and fake images had been posted online without Parker's consent. She was the victim of a rancorous, sustained coordinated attack so humiliating, dehumanizing, and threatening that she withdrew socially, became clinically depressed, and coped through behaviors that developed into addictions. Yet still, she did not think she deserved to complain. What's more, she believes that if she had complained, it would not have helped.

Like others, Parker is assessing her abuse through the individual-attack lens used by police, platforms, and many employers. In the process, she reduces the severity of the profoundly toxic attacks leveled against her into a single, fairly tepid insult. Make no mistake, Parker is outraged by her attack and feels strongly that women need better protections, but she is not immune to dismissive, minimizing discourses about what counts as abuse. This is, after all, her culture too. Frustrated, she confessed,

As I'm speaking this to you, I actually feel shame because I feel like there's this whole idea of, "Well, it's just the Internet." It just keeps coming up, over and over again. "Well, it's just the Internet. Why do you care? It's just the Internet." There is a part of me, even right now saying this to you, saying, "Why did I get depressed? That's dumb."

Parker hesitates about seeking help. She feels ashamed for having been upended by the torment. She feels like she's the problem.

Nearly every woman I spoke with downplayed her experiences with digital attacks. Several used the most high-profile cases from the news as reference points, qualifying their attacks as less horrible than the attacks faced by other women. Anita Sarkeesian, Zoe Quinn, and Brianna Wu of Gamergate came up most frequently in these comparisons. Other women whose digital backlash made the news were cited, too—journalist Amy Hess, author Lindy West, programmer Kathy Sierra, broadcaster Katy Tur, and comedian Leslie Jones among them. It was as if the respondents assumed I would think their experience frivolous unless they had been forced to hire bodyguards, lost their jobs, or been driven into hiding. Here are a just handful of examples:

Sophia: I mean, I've had it easy, compared to a lot of people I know.

Ruby: The first round was primarily, "You're a dumb bitch, you know nothing." "Fucking don't talk about sports because you're an idiot." "Women are stupid" kind of stuff. Like the word cunt or whatever, just stuff like that, which could have been sent to anybody. . . .[W]hat I got wasn't as vitriolic as what I've seen them [women in the headlines] get, for sure.

Tori: Some people might go after me on Twitter, but I didn't receive nearly the level of abuse that some other people did.

Maria: I feel like it could be worse. . . . I bet Katy Tur at NBC got a lot worse during the [Trump] campaign.

Jennifer: I would say that there are women who are attacked in a really much worse way.

Esther: This is happening and I knew so many feminist writers who are being threatened with rape. It happens on all the platforms. I've gotten threats on Tumblr, on Facebook, on Twitter. The threats, I don't get a lot of threats the way some people do.

Most remarkably, even respondents whose own harassment made the news downplayed their abuse, pointing out that digital harassment is just de rigueur in the worlds they inhabit.

The prevalence of digital toxicity and these women's awareness of it could certainly increase their outrage—and it does. All but one of my interviewees described digital sexism and abuse as profoundly unjust and the inability of police, platforms, and employers to prevent them as unacceptable. And yet, their principled resistance was generally reserved for abuse as an abstract phenomenon and for their assessments of *other* women's hardships. When it came to their own attacks, there was considerably more ambivalence. As I listened to women scrutinize and diminish their own experiences with the cold objectivity of imagined judges, trivializing narratives loomed large; they were determined to complain only when they believe an assault would align with the policies and popular narratives regarding what is deemed legitimately upsetting.

Going It Alone

Some respondents, including Hazel and Esther, actively fight the hostile climate online (see Chapter 4). Most respondents' accounts, however, revealed a marked contrast between their willful rejection digital toxicity as acceptable and their resignation to withstanding that environment, even if it means managing the toxicity on their own. More than half of my participants described digital abuse matter-of-factly as an unavoidable reality in their lives. Jan is a wise-cracking, self-effacing White lesbian in her 30s, who has made her career as a political pundit, columnist, and author. In an uncharacteristic moment of solemnity, Jan sighed, "I've accepted it as the price of doing business in the business that I'm in at this moment in history. But it is relentlessly unpleasant." Rina agrees, considering digital abuse a side-effect of her career path: "I had to sort of prepare myself for the possibility that I could get doxxed, and that was scary—sort of realizing the personal ramifications of the career choices that I've made."

Among those who were openly pessimistic about the possibility for positive change, Maria, a well-known, White fact-checker in her 30s, was sanguine: "I realized pretty quickly when I started fact-checking—that I would have to develop a pretty tough skin to do this kind of work. I feel like I have. I think the gender stuff is just something we have to deal with as women. I just don't see the world becoming a more sensitive, egalitarian place any time super-soon."

Scarlett, the academic and game designer, felt hopeless. With her characteristic descriptive color, she depicted this rampant abuse as something society has decided to live with.

> I think, sometimes, I think it's some kind of a Rabelais thing, where instead of the carnival being a release of order and a topsy-turvy moment, instead, it's a moment of order. We have this complete sea of terrifying chaos and we get a moment of order and someone is fired or someone is arrested or someone is told, "You can't post death threats on the internet, because it's not okay," but that's it. It's a moment, and then done, like it exorcised all of our rights to have any kind of safety. . . . I don't see any concrete steps being taken to address this. I think a lot of organizations, nonprofits, government stuff, companies, they're willing to pump some money into it, and so it looks like they're trying to do something, but I don't see it [changing].

It is little wonder that, in the end, women on the receiving end of digital attacks feel they are in this alone. Existing US legal options and social media platform policies fail women with attacker and attack-focused accountability systems incapable of addressing the broad, climate-level issues with which women struggle. Making matters worse, cultural beliefs that trivialize women's experiences through victim-blaming, disregard for nonphysical harm, and the untenable assumption that it is not worth getting worked up over something that is "just" online form a mythology that even affects women's sense of the abuse they endure. Structural negligence and cultural scripts leave women with a justifiable sense that they have little recourse and are on their own (or at least, on their own together). They strategize and adapt, commiserating with peers, working on developing a thicker skin, or figuring out how to get out of harm's way. The harm simply continues.

3

Constant Calibration
(Preventative Labor)

Although the substance of these attacks is predictable—drawing on sexist, racist, xenophobic, and homophobic tropes that have been in place for hundreds of years—their frequency and intensity can be erratic. This uncertainty leaves women determined to manage the few details that remain in their control, in hopes of avoiding abuse. Trying to prevent harassment involves undertaking time-consuming and emotionally draining efforts to narrow the scope and impact of would-be attacks. The women I interviewed described four main approaches to managing their abuse: they work to improve their digital security, consult their mental maps of riskier and safer digital spaces, monitor their emotional stamina to assess whether they are "up to" participation, and engage extensive credibility-work designed to limit attackers' ability to discredit or shame them.

Rituals of Safekeeping

These harm-avoidance behaviors are familiar. They are direct analogs to the protective repertoires women undertake to avoid unwanted sexual attention and violence in other public spaces. "Safety checklists" of things women feel (or are told) they should do—and not to do—to manage risk have been well documented (Frazier and Falmagne 2014). Research shows, for instance, that young women going out at night follow a series of "rules" such as avoiding certain venues or types of venues, watching their drinks closely, and establishing predetermined SOS signals with friends should they need help (Graham et al. 2017; Fileborn 2016). Other studies document similar safety protocols

Credible Threat. Sarah Sobieraj, Oxford University Press (2020). © Oxford University Press.
DOI: 10.1093/oso/9780190089283.001.0001.

used by women in nature: not going alone, carrying whistles or mace, varying routes, and staying away after dusk (Wesely and Gaarder 2004; Roper 2016). During the day, women's strategies to avoid harm involve consciously altering schedules and traveling in groups to minimize risk when using public transportation (Loukaitou-Sideris 2014; d'Arbois de Jubainville and Vanier 2017; Kash 2019). And at work, women have tried to avoid sexual harassment through strategic dress, restricting the way the use their bodies (e.g., not bending over), and steering clear of particular colleagues, clients, or patrons (Denissen 2010; Hughes and Tadic 1998). These harm-avoidance strategies map onto canards of sexual assault prevention advice suggesting that avoiding sexual violence is women's responsibility. In many cases these techniques are ineffective, in light of the vast amount of violence that occurs in private settings and is perpetrated by people known to their victims (Larsen, Hilden, and Lidegaard 2015; Bedera and Nordmeyer 2015; Stanko 1993; Gardner 1990; RAINN 2017).

These repertoires help to manage fear of sexual violence by allowing women to feel more in control and less anxious (Silva and Wright 2009). Such coping mechanisms have emerged in response to several factors. These include personal experiences with sexual harassment and violence (street harassment, digital attacks, sexual assault, etc.), the awareness that the prevalence of violence against women places them at continued risk, neoliberal ideology that blames victims for irresponsible decision making, and the absence of meaningful legal or cultural pressure to hold men accountable for their violence, despite decades of advocacy work intended to close these gaps. The women in this sample are well aware that following the rules does not ensure safety, but they also feel determined to do what little they can—short of leaving digital publics altogether—in the face of a phenomenon that makes them feel powerless.

TAKING DIGITAL SECURITY PRECAUTIONS

Women's preventative labor involves attempting to stave off attacks and to mitigate potential harm. Many spoke of working to improve their digital security to help them better contain any subsequent damage. Several women told me they feared hackers might try to obtain their personal information or hijack their social media accounts, so they made modest efforts such as setting up discrete, automatically generated passwords for each account, changing passwords frequently, and using two-factor authentication. Others took security measures linked to their physical safety, including limiting or turning off geolocation settings on their phones or location-tagging on social media platforms such as Instagram, Snapchat, and Twitter. A handful protected their long-standing phone numbers from doxxing attacks by setting up Google Voice numbers that relayed their calls to the "real" phone numbers. Willa, the young woman whose social media account was hacked in a coordinated attack, set up an email relay system to divert potential abuse:

> Like on my CV too, I have a dummy account essentially. . . . And now anytime I publish my email address online, I'm using that account. It filters into a different folder, so that if I am ever undergoing sustained harassment in the future, I can defer that out of my inbox, and check it periodically, but not have to compromise the integrity of my email inbox.

Lynette, the public intellectual, enlisted her IT professionals to prevent abusive email from flooding her inbox:

> I did learn, when I was still at [my previous university], when I was about to publish something that I thought might spark something, I started reaching out to the IT department to say, "Listen. Can you all just tweak my spam filter for a little bit? This thing is probably going to happen." That was one of my solutions.

Some women trawled the internet for personal information about themselves and removed it to bolster their sense of safety. Some methodically deleted information related to their home and office addresses, for example. A couple of women took down entire blogs, explaining that they had been written at a time when they believed they could be freer online. Karen, a White female Wikipedia editor in her 60s, went so far as to hire a privacy protection service to remove her identifying information from data broker sites such as Addresses.com and Spokeo.

Fatima, the freelance journalist, had been guarded about what she revealed online from the outset: "The first advice I got was, 'Don't share anything personal. Like don't even have your photo on your Twitter account. Don't share anything personal.'" When I asked who gave her that advice, she said,

Other women. Other women that [said] "Just be careful." And actually, I had a male tell me as well. I had a family member say, "Don't share anything." . . . I don't share my kids' faces or photos, I just don't do that. Even though my son is on Twitter, I don't share his tweets, because his entire profile is about his school, and so people can locate us very quickly, geographically.

Grace, the investigative reporter, is also an activist. She decided to go back and edit her online presence once she started to become more visible. She feared critics of her public work around reproductive rights would use that information to come after her and her family:

At the end of that summer, we did seven weeks of protesting, and it got more and more contentious as we went. And by the end of that I had gone through and deleted every picture of my [child] that existed online and tried to make sure that his name did not show up anywhere. . . . I was going on vacation. . . . I didn't know what kind of internet I'd have when I got there, what kind of access. I remember sitting in the [local] airport and just deleting every picture on Facebook of my child. And I had a blog that I don't know if anyone could have found if I hadn't given them the link, but it was still public. And I had blogged pictures of my son for my parents to follow for the first couple years of [his] life. I locked that down. I think I eventually just deleted the whole thing. I think I went through and deleted every Tweet. I don't know if I've ever used his name on Twitter, but I would try to get rid of anything that would identify him because by the time [the high-profile activism] was over, there were very angry anti-choice people who did not like me and were digging into me to see if I had gotten paid to do what I had done, as if that would matter. Just invasive stuff that made me nervous, and I didn't want it to spill over onto my kid in any way. So that was the first time I remember taking active measures to protect myself and my family because of the response. . . . I just had a very high profile by the time it was over. . . . [Counter-protesters] would take my picture. . . . [W]e all felt intimidated. . . . I would be on camera, I would be interviewed for local news or whatever, and people would come up just behind the camera and they'd get very close because you can't move, right, when you're on camera. So they'd get really close to me. The whole thing was just a lot and I felt easily recognizable by the time we got to the end of that period. . . . Then there was a blog post about me and maybe one other person and it was like, "Who is this person? Are they being paid? Why are they doing this?" Just questions that made me very nervous coming from that particular person. . . . That was the first time I remember thinking I should [take pre-emptive efforts].

Activists often want and need visibility, but that visibility is also a burden. Grace hoped removing her personal information would reduce potential damage should her critics decide to lash out against her. But eliminating private information can be stressful. Most adults have years of accumulated internet history and it is not easy to put that toothpaste back in the tube. As Grace described sitting in that airport, frantically deleting digital information about her child, I could hear the fear and anxiety rise in her voice. In that moment, she felt she was racing to get to the photos before her attackers could weaponize them.

Mental Maps of the Digital Terrain

Witnessing the calibrations made by the women in this research—their attempts to construct and carve out safe, or at least safer, uses of digital publics—calls to mind Gill Valentine's research on the geography of women's fear. In her groundbreaking work, we learn that the fear of male violence leads women to avoid "dangerous places" at "dangerous times." It restricts the way women and other vulnerable groups use public spaces. The women in her study used an array of indicators to assess safety, preferring, for example, public spaces perceived as formally controlled (patrolled by police, security guards, and others in positions of authority) or at least informally monitored (e.g., places where neighbors are accessible if needed). Parents, Valentine argues, socialize female children into restricting their movement because they worry for girls in a context of media reporting about violence against women and their own lived experiences of harassment (1989, 385–88).

It is striking how similar the women in this research sound as they describe their judicious assessments of which platforms to use, which communities within a particular platform to enter, and how or when it is safe for them to speak in different venues. Like Valentine's respondents' preference for formal control, the women in this research prefer digital publics with reporting features, comment moderation, and other affordances that provide a buffer between them and those who might lash out. This came up repeatedly in interviews, as women contrasted good places with bad ones in terms of how the platforms handled abusive content.

The spaces that my participants identified as most dangerous were described as free-for-alls, whereas digital spaces considered low-risk tended to moderate comments tightly—or dispense with commenting all together. Fatima had been chastised for this preference and resented the critique: "People are like, 'Oh, well that's censorship!' No, it's really easy to say that's censorship. It's also about an outlet protecting their writers and their journalists. And as a freelancer, I feel that more because I'm not on staff so I have basically no protection at all." In other words, professionally and personally, a lack of moderation makes Fatima feel unsafe.

Major social media platforms, which do not offer the pre-emptive moderation provided by many newspapers and blogs, were seen as riskier spaces, though not as risky as Reddit, 4Chan, 8Chan, and rumor mill discussion boards such as AutoAdmit. Those were universally and consistently coded as dangerous. The women I spoke with have varied, if clear, personal preferences among sites such as Facebook, YouTube, Instagram, Twitter, and Tumblr.

Colu is a calm and tentative Black freelance journalist in her 20s who has been stung by online attacks on several occasions. She spoke at length about her preference for platforms that de-emphasize interaction and where participants are less likely to be anonymous:

> If it's [a video] that I'm going to appear in, and then I get—especially if it's going on somewhere like YouTube and I'd say Facebook, [where] the comments can just be awful. . . . And so, I'd say if it's something that is video where I will be appearing in it, and it's going to be on somewhere like YouTube or Facebook, it can be particularly bad. Twitter can be bad, but I'd say Facebook and YouTube more so in my experience. Because I think those kind[s] of communities, they emphasize commenting, don't they? . . . Yeah. But . . . especially on YouTube, if you leave a comment, you're not necessarily going to be directed to the profile of someone where you'd get a lot of information about them. So, it's much more rooted in anonymity really. Isn't it? Like, going to someone's YouTube profile, you'll probably not get a lot of identifying information about them. On Twitter, if it's a burner

account, that's a bit weird. Do you know what I mean? . . . Like, all these egg accounts. Nobody knows who it is, but on YouTube it's much more acceptable to be this anonymous account that doesn't really post.

Twitter feels safer than YouTube to Colu, but many women in my sample thought Twitter felt decidedly unsafe. Opinions varied, shaped heavily by factors such as their number of followers, friends, or subscribers on a given platform; the ideological and social diversity of those consuming their content; and the women's prior experiences on the platform. Fiona, a queer, multiracial vlogger in her 20s, tailored her content according to her perception of the risk posed by the platform where it would appear. Relatable and wry, Fiona has almost 100,000 subscribers who tune in to her YouTube channel for her weekly, earnest social analyses related to race, gender, sexuality, and mental health, but, to her, Tumblr feels safer:

> I monitor myself more on places I know I'm going to get more back-lash and more abuse. I feel like I need to make stronger arguments [on YouTube], and it almost doesn't allow for as much vulnerability. I'm like, anything I say that's in the slightest bit open, it's going to make it easier for other people to attack that. I'm much more open on other websites, like Tumblr, where I know people don't generally go on my Tumblr and leave 20 abusive comments. It'll happen once in a blue moon, but I feel safer there. I feel like I can open up and be more honest and more myself to talk about other things I don't feel as comfortable talking about on YouTube. I don't have to feel as guarded or defensive [on those platforms].

Fiona tries to protect herself in higher risk venues by being more guarded about the content she posts.

The women I interviewed also revealed a preference for spaces where like-minded peers function as digital neighbors. Sometimes these digital neighbors are people they know are ready to chime in and provide support if things get ugly, by chiding critics or posting supportive content. At other times, women assess the norms and culture of the neighborhood itself before they decide to participate. Casey, the expert on technology, sports, and gaming, explained the factors she thinks about when gaming and writing online:

I also am pretty intentional about the guilds I pick to join. I ask about harassment policies. I ask [about] their language . . . so I think a lot of us who just, you know, like I think we are often, intentional about where we spend time, if we can be . . . I would not want my story to be one of choices that protected me [from more severe attacks], but it's more like, here are strategies I do to minimize the opportunities [for abuse] with full recognition that shit happens, despite all of our best efforts, and I can't explain why it happens to one person and not another.

Preventative care then transfers to physical spaces, as a result of identity-based attacks online. For example, at the height of the most intense abuse, Hazel had security guards and even bomb-sniffing dogs to make sure that the physical spaces in which she gave public talks were safe. Lynette no longer posts information about upcoming speaking engagements on her website, and Rina describes being on high alert when she speaks publicly:

The first thing I do whenever I'm giving a public talk, or whenever I'm giving a talk in a space where I'm not entirely sure, I scan the room. I scan the room for threat. I try to figure out who the [threat] in the room might be and what they might say and what they might do. I'm very, very hyper aware when I give talks right now, and I'm sure I will be as my next book is published. To me, [entering the room] is . . . the anxiety provoking moment.

This sounds very much like an account a woman might have shared with Gill Valentine about walking alone at night: scanning for threat, being hyper aware. The parallels are extensive. Importantly, though, there *is* a discrepancy between the way women manage physical and digital public spaces. In dangerous digital publics, women can be attacked *even if they are not present*. Several of the women I spoke with described monitoring "bad places" they avoided, having deemed them too dangerous. They believed they might be targeted in those venues.

Tori, a prolific White academic in her 40s, has spoken publicly and critically about gaming. She was targeted by a multi-platform coordinated attack. Because of her experiences and the headline-grabbing stories of abuse wrought by gamers against critics, Tori felt a need to watch digital spaces where she was not active, just to keep an eye out for potential threats. She described monitoring 8chan:

> It's just every kind of the most ridiculous, racist, sexist, homophobic statements that you can find, are there. The way that people address each other is on this board, it was like "fags" and "hey faggot," and "I'm the lead faggot." And this is the normal language. And so if you're not used to it, just the language that they use, even if it's not about you, is really overwhelming. So getting used to that, getting used to how they use it, the images and the memes, and the way that people will just argue for things even if they don't necessarily believe it. So it takes a certain amount of, I don't know, stomach to be able to just look at it in general. And then to look at it, and you're looking, asking, "Is my name going to be here? Or are there the names of people I know . . . going to appear here?"

Again, like the participants in Valentine's (1989) research, the women I spoke with had been socialized into their surveillant and restrictive practices. They learned these behaviors through warnings and advice delivered by those who have been attacked or are aware of others who have been attacked (consider the warnings Fatima described above), news coverage that highlights cases of extreme attacks (Tori explicitly told me that she was wary of ending up targeted as Anita Sarkeesian or Zoe Quinn were during GamerGate), and their own experiences of identity-based pushback online (Fiona learned which platforms were more abusive by wading into them).

SELF-SCRUTINY

In addition to carefully evaluating digital and physical spaces for safety risks, women also monitor themselves. I found that women assess whether they are "up to" the toxic backlash that might result from their participation. This mode of preventative work is not about reducing the amount of abuse but assessing the amount of harm that might come from abuse directed at them. Women repeatedly described performing self-assessment, at times working to manage their own emotions so that they could get themselves in a place where they felt they could hit send or publish.

It might be difficult, if you have not been targeted by identity-based attacks online, to imagine that publishing, speaking, or posting might be "rewarded" with abuse. Yet this awareness looms over the women I spoke with as they work. For Lynette, the emotional impact of the gender- and race-based harassment with which she has grown so familiar does not keep her from expressing her ideas in writing, but sometimes it keeps her from sharing her opinions, insights, and ideas publicly:

> I write. I was writing whether anyone was reading or not. That's just what I do. It is hard and hurtful for me when I have to think about not writing. When I . . . question whether I should write . . . I've got a couple of things that I wrote and then when I looked at it, I put it away. I thought, "No." Now, it's either I'm tired or it's a bad point in my life or it's a great point in my life and I just don't feel like having this right now, because I know what will happen. . . . I know it will happen, and I don't have the mental reserves to do it. I put it away. That bothers me because I hope I never let it [the potential for harassment] change what I write or how I write but, I think it would be naive of me think that it hasn't.

Self-censorship is explored more fully in Chapter 5, but Lynette's assessment of what she calls her "mental reserves" is important here because it is *work* to constantly undertake this kind of internal debate. For Lynette, the writing seems to come easily. The struggle comes when she considers whether to share it publicly.

Liz is a White blogger in her 20s who writes about mental health, sexual assault, and popular culture. Her own mental health has been impacted by the gender-based attacks she's endured in response to her writing, and Liz has a great deal of trepidation about discussing social issues online. Sounding discouraged, she told me she never wrote anything—even comments—in a public space without internal turmoil:

> If I'm going to comment on something, frequently, it has to do with calling out some sort of slut-shaming, or other problematic gender issue, and I have to think about how much blow-back am I going to get from this, and how much is it worth it to me? . . . Anytime I'm commenting on something serious, which is pretty much the only time I will step out of my comfort zone and comment somewhere on the internet that's not my friend's blog posts, it's a real dialogue I have with myself about if it's worth it. Usually it's not worth it. At

the end of the day, I have to put my mental well-being first, and it's a debate that you have to have with yourself about "what is the cost of the potential reaction of this versus what is the value of empowerment that I get when my [perspective] is valid and is [no longer] missing from this dialog?"

The content Liz feels most compelled to contribute—to call attention to gender inequality—is, in her experience, the most likely to illicit ugly responses. She feels torn much of the time but told me that she is most likely to accept that risk when she believes she can potentially change or open others' minds. Lucy, the science and technology journalist, described a similar moment of calculation when she was torn between writing a piece on gender-based harassment that was very important to her and worrying that the subsequent backlash might be more than she could handle. She told me, "I think that's the worst thing about it. It's this idea that I kind of feel exhausted about the prospect [of doing the story]. Even that piece I was like, I don't know if I can be bothered to deal with the associated shit. . . . I was sort of reticent to publish on that topic."

Esther, the media critic, takes her own emotional temperature before putting her work out there. At times, she threads the needle, deciding to publish but attempting to limit the audience to friendlier readers. "In the past, I've asked editors, I've said things like, 'Hey, can you please change that headline, because I don't have the emotional wherewithal right now to deal with the blow-back that it's going to cause me if the conservative media picks that up.' I, personally, know that."

CONSTRUCTING UNASSAILABILITY

In the introduction I described attacks intent on discrediting women as particularly prevalent. It is of little surprise, then, that in addition to beefing up security, appraising the safety of public venues, and monitoring on their own emotional and mental bandwidth, women invest tremendous time and energy into "credibility work" they hope will help protect them from digital harassment. By "credibility work," I mean the range of strategies they use to prove that they are people whose ideas are worth hearing. Women showcase their status, expertise, accuracy, objectivity, and respectability, banking them as currency that might limit the efficacy of discrediting attacks.

These efforts prove important in a context where women's voices are often discounted. Sophia, the business news editor, became animated with frustration when she described a Facebook discussion about current affairs:

> There was one fairly obnoxious guy, who had commented on one of the news stories she [a friend] had put up, and I, sort of, responded with a different viewpoint. It was a funny thing, because he immediately got so incredibly incensed, and kind of, like, lost it—right away. He responded with something that didn't make a lot of sense and I tried to shut down the conversation, but he sort of . . . I don't know how else to put it. It was like a rabid dog. He started, like, foaming at the mouth, via social media. And ended up, through about probably 12 different posts, I mean, calling me . . . He called me a bimbo. He called me stupid. He called me a slut. And then, he would alternate between that and saying, "Come on, Madame Professor, Why don't you thrill me with all the academic texts you've ever published? Here are mine." I mean, it was crazy. . . [H]e called me a sniveling [tramp], which was a new one. I'm like, I'm not even sure what that means. But it was an absolute meltdown. . . . So, after this was over, I have an incredibly smart attorney friend [Walter], and . . . he chimed in and, basically, said the same thing to this guy that I had said in the first place. The guy responded to him, "Thank you, [Walter], for your interesting thoughts. I was just responding to X, Y, and Z, X, Y, and Z, with Sophia . . ." It was so striking to me that the tone of deference and just conversation, to a guy . . . versus how he immediately became aggressive and abusive and disgusting and sexist [with me].

Rather than challenge Sophia's substantive claims—which would mark her as a legitimate interlocutor—this aggressor asserted that her perspective could not be taken seriously. *How many books had she written on the subject?* he asked, provocatively, calling her a stupid bimbo, taunting and belittling her at once. Sophia's account is instructive, because it reminds us that identity-based attacks are often coupled with other insults that are not explicitly identity-based (bimbo, for instance, accompanies stupid). Still, even those challenges that *appear* non-gendered are lobbed more often at women (and presumably those who do not identify as women but hail from other marginalized groups). As Sophia elaborated, "[Walter] is met with complete and total, sort of, deference and respect for his opinion, and I was called a bimbo."

Many times, I heard about male colleagues, co-authors, and supervisors stunned to learn the brutality of the feedback directed at their female counterparts. Grace said,

> One of my best friends is [a male colleague], and I wrote [a piece] with [him] . . . a couple years ago. I retweeted him, something like that, and so he got the responses. . . . And he was like, "Holy shit, is this your life? Is this how people respond to you all the time when you tweet?" And I was like, "Yeah, is this weird?" And so part of [what surprised him] was just the volume of it, but also the correcting you kind of part. Like making sure you're right all the time.

Women weren't afforded slack in the way men were. Even having written academic books on a given subject does not insulate women from credibility challenges. Rina, a credentialed and widely published academic, had similar experiences. She described one in particular:

> I was like, "Here's 350 words on why I think this is kind of interesting and something to talk about and a reason why we need to think differently about it." That got some [unpleasant] response, and I really regretted writing it. Like *really* regretted writing it. . . . Some of it was just people on Twitter calling me stupid, saying "she doesn't know what the fuck she's talking about, how did anyone give her a degree in anything," blah, blah, blah. . . . It was pure attack. It was like, "you're stupid, you stupid bitch, how is it that you . . . You don't know anything about anything. You don't know what you're talking about."

Commenters on Fiona's vlogs are similarly devoted to dissecting the accuracy of her assertions:

> I don't feel if I'm going to talk about sexual harassment, I need to make a fool-proof argument about it and look up tons of specifics. Obviously, there's a time and a place for that and it's important. Sometimes I just want to be able to share my experiences without having to cite 20 specific studies and sources. I feel like I can't do that . . . because it's going to be ripped apart. . . . I'll have people that if I don't cite . . . If I say, "Women experience sexual harassment," even something very general, something that you can easily find online.

Stuff I would take as something that's obvious—that as a woman, we can get sexually harassed, or yes, women experience rape culture. Other people, like men, 100% men who don't have those experiences to back that up, and are not familiar with research and studies, and other women talking about that kind of thing, they'll come in and think, "This is just your opinion. I need hard facts and research. Your experience doesn't matter because it's not accompanied with science." . . . It's like, "You're just a woman. What you're saying isn't worthwhile or credible until you prove this."

These incessant challenges were eating away at Fiona:

The overall intent is [to say] "Your voice doesn't matter. What you have to say is not valuable. It doesn't mean anything. It doesn't change anything. You might as well not have said anything at all." There is that sense of what I say matters less. I feel like my opinions and my experiences get devalued by these kinds of comments. It does take a hit to your self-esteem, and you start thinking, "Maybe I didn't have anything worthwhile to say. Maybe I shouldn't have said anything at all." It's hard to think that this isn't intentional.

Cheryl is a deliberate and confident White woman in her 50s. She is a high-profile long-form journalist, and her writing has appeared in many national magazines and newspapers. Over the years, she told me, she learned that her work would be subject to intense sexist scrutiny. In response, she became exacting:

Unfortunately in our world, demeaning women through sexualization is tried and true. It's worked for years. . . . [W]hen you dare to step into a complicated realm, you have to be reduced by being sexualized. . . . There are a lot of subtleties and it's a lot of work to do complex stories, because you know you may be attacked and you just have to really go down every avenue to make sure you have it right. . . . I always try to get things right, but definitely when you're writing about something that you know is either highly technical or highly emotional or both—or if it has a lot of different constituencies, covers a lot of different very strongly held feelings or has a gendered element to it . . . if you're a woman writing about it . . . you're

triple, double, triple checking. You're checking people. You're checking people who you recorded the interview to say, "Is this really what
you meant? I have it here, I just transcribed it, you did say it. . . . Did
you mean it like this? Because I really want to be sure that you meant
it like that."

This determination to root out anything that could possibly be misconstrued
or seen as erroneous also came up in my interview with Esther, who said her
expertise was challenged "every single day." While discussing about what she
described as "extremely, extremely careful and constrained editing," Esther
explained:

> Credibility is an issue in general for women. I'm not an academic.
> Some women arm themselves, for good reason, with their academic
> accomplishments, because it's the only way to get themselves heard—
> and even that doesn't necessarily work. I feel that very much. I'm like,
> "Okay. So, I'm a thinker and a writer, and it's just my opinion. Okay."
> Like, "Yes, I have studied extensively what I'm talking about." . . . [But]
> I feel very strongly that I can't afford to make mistakes. That's how
> I feel, right? The price for making any mistake is so high that I'm just
> super careful. Especially talking about things like rape, which is why
> in my work, I tend to profusely cite and link: because I don't want to
> argue with morons. "If you have a problem, go talk to the CDC and
> the Department of Justice and the UN and have a nice day."

Of course, accuracy is important, essential even, to journalists and activists.
But Cheryl and Esther have learned that the price of an error is degradation,
personal attacks, gendered epithets, and intimidation, when it should be a
reminder about fact-checking from an editor or a matter of simple clarification.

Cat, the sports analyst, was so acutely aware that her identity would warp
how her work was received that the need for credibility shaped her professional choices from the outset:

> I decided when I wanted to start writing about [sports] . . . that I was
> going to go in the statistical, analytical direction. [It] was because
> I didn't want to leave room to not be taken seriously as a writer
> because I am a woman. I wanted, I guess, a foundation that could not
> be shaken as a result of my gender. Before I started [writing in this

space], when I lurked around the edges of the [sports] Twitter community, which, for basically all intents and purposes, is where journalists and fans and individual bloggers and writers all interact in this, what sometimes can be called honestly, a cesspool. I got the sense that I just needed that ability to say, "My work is factually correct."

Cat knew statistics were not enough to insulate her in the digital sphere, and so she engaged in an array of credibility work. She intentionally wore glasses in her professional photo, "[I thought,] try to look as professional as possible. Don't attract the attention of people who might say that stuff." And in a sea of what she called "slap-dash" analytics work presented without even basic contextualizing information (e.g., information about how data were collected or should be interpreted), she tried to anticipate every possible question or critique. Still, Cat said, her efforts were unsuccessful: "It does go to show that—despite the armor that I had begun to construct at that point in time, it was still obviously not impervious. People were still seeing me as a gendered, sexualized person or object, and that was deeply uncomfortable." Similarly, in the context of talking about all the care and deliberation that goes into her work, Grace sighed, "But the reality of it is, is that I can be as accurate as I can possibly ever be, and still there will be blow-back."

Hope is at the heart of all credibility work—hope that listeners, viewers, or readers might take what these women have to say seriously. These efforts are a way of asking not to be dismissed or undermined. This means that the types of credibility work that are seen as effective (at least, somewhat effective) are context dependent. Alex, the academic and avid political tweeter, performed credibility work around her political identity. To signal that she was unbiased and relatable, she commented on her blue-collar roots, referenced familial relationships to law enforcement, and asserted her patriotism. Her hope was that by signaling a tendency toward political centrism, she could stave off being discredited as, in her words, a "flaming liberal bitchface." Even so, Alex mocked her own attempts: "My thought is, 'Oh, maybe they will see that they're mischaracterizing my place in the world.' But they don't care!" She continued, "As soon as I start going down that path"—of trying to prove she is unbiased—"I end up regretting it. Because they don't care! They don't care. They don't care!"

Sometimes women feel they need to alter their appearance to be credible, as we saw with by Cat and her glasses. Some were afraid to look too attractive or too young or too feminine. Taken to its extreme, it can feel as though in order to be credible, it is best not to be female at all. Aubrey and Anastasia each occasionally change their avatars to images of White men to get a break from the abuse. Both women found the difference striking. Aubrey noted that the abuse did decrease significantly, as she had hoped, but the change in how her ideas were received was far more surprising:

> When I changed my profile picture to a man, most of [the harassment] stopped. . . . And people also took me more seriously, which was kind of funny, like people who didn't realize that I wasn't a man, even people that were being nice, were less likely to try and explain things to me or argue with me. Actually, a few people that I'm friendly with, nice people online, then wrote to me and they were like, "Oh my god, I really hate to admit this, but for some reason I take you more seriously, and I just noticed that about myself, and just thanks for doing this."

While Aubrey and Anastasia intermittently used White male faces as masks, Alex distanced femininity as part of her ongoing legitimacy strategy. Alex is a feminine cis-woman, and she is conventionally attractive. She wears makeup, has shoulder-length hair that she styles, and to an outsider presents herself in ways that conform to gender expectations. And yet, when Alex wants people to recognize her expertise, femininity becomes a burden that she rejects mentally and physically. She worked through her ideas and feelings about this as we spoke:

> Is it weird if I say that when I navigate [digital and physical spaces where she wants to be taken seriously], in my mind I *am* male? . . . When I'm in those spaces, I do not think of myself as a woman at all. At all. At all. At all. I think of myself as a suit. I'm in a suit. I'm wearing a suit. . . . When I'm in front of students, when I teach my classes, when I show up on media, or whatever, I do not want a gender. I just want to be a suit who's talking. . . . Online, I don't want a gender. Yeah. . . . I did an interview that was a 20-minute long interview on TV, where I was interviewed by a male. When I watched it, I was like, "Oh, I think I dropped the octave of my voice a little bit." I did that. I seemed really serious. And this is maybe why, like we've talked about, I really don't like television interviews, because I feel like I completely transform. . . . When I present my research,

if I present for students, I think that I'm more of an androgynous version of myself, but I don't "go male." However, I did do a presentation for a room full of wealthy financial industry folks that were largely male, and in that room, I think I did drop my octave, and I just remember feeling like, "Here I am, talking about this thing. I'm an expert. Look at me. I'm an expert." Yeah . . . It's more about how I feel like I will be perceived. It's not about what is true. Of course women can be experts. Women are super experts, and they're wicked fucking smart! But it's about how we're perceived. I feel like, if you show up on TV and you're too pretty, you are not smart. I definitely feel that. Which is super shitty to say, right? Yeah.

Rejecting femininity did not mean cutting her hair or forgoing makeup. Instead, for Alex, it was about shifting her way of being in the world. It was a shift in the way she used space, commanded attention, wielded confidence, and persisted against intellectual challenges. It showed up in the way she spoke, in both the pitch of her voice and her rejection of apologies and qualifiers. It meant changing how she carried herself. Alex did not feel a need to "go male" in order to be given respect in the classroom, but in her male-dominated discipline, in her meetings with male industry executives, in her interviews with established male broadcasters, and in her tweets, she used masculinity— at least, the most socially valued forms of masculinity—as a tool.

Indeed, these strategies are common among women endeavoring to be seen as professional and competent, though they are often unaware as they lower their voices or choose a blazer and eschew a scarf for a public appearance. This form of credibility work speaks more directly to the foundations of gender-based harassment—power and inequality—than the forms emphasizing fastidiousness on accuracy, political ideology, or physical appearance. It is an attempt at commanding attention as an erudite expert, a role historically denied women because they have long been devalued.

Rules and Tools and Work

These proactive adaptations help women feel more secure in an obstinately unpredictable, threatening space that is simultaneously too valuable to reject. They also come with their own costs. The work required to try to close the gendered digital safety gap is not evenly distributed but an onus placed squarely on women. It is a draining response to an already exhausting problem. That is, those who stand to suffer most from an onslaught of abuse suffer most from their attempts to mitigate such vitriol. For example, women who work as freelancers, academics, pundits, and activists; those who are younger, not yet established, or lack job security; and politicians whose careers hinge on the way others view them are inescapably aware that digital toxicity could be their professional undoing. These women do not have the luxury of ignoring or laughing off content that impugns them or their work. This is less true of women who have well-established reputations, job security, and employers who can help them manage some of the hostility.

And, of course, just as we know that women who avoid going out at night and dress modestly are still sexually assaulted, there is no amount of preventative work that ensures safe participation in digital publics. Safety is not created by wearing a pair of glasses or adding academic credentials to a Twitter bio. It will require changing the cultures that ignore and even promote digital toxicity. Without such structural change, women will not only labor to stave off attacks but also work to endure and cope when attacks transpire in spite of their efforts. This struggle to cope is the subject of Chapter 4.

4

Anger Management
(Ameliorative Labor)

As with other forms of gendered abuse, following victim-avoidance "rules" does not ensure safety for women who speak publicly about political and social issues online. Even those who judiciously calibrate their behavior are often attacked, and the obscene, humiliating, and frightening messages they receive can be profoundly disturbing. To buoy themselves and preserve their willingness to participate in digital publics, women cope. Remember Debbie, the sardonic political pundit and nonprofit executive? As you may recall, she has a long history of receiving vitriolic, graphic, and intimidating attacks. Among the safety precautions she takes, Debbie has relocated her office and had a panic button installed, walks to her car with an emergency app open on her phone, and remains in regular contact with someone at the Federal Bureau of Investigation (FBI). Even so, Debbie says she is unfazed by the harassment. She did not mince words in our interview: "It doesn't bother me," she said plainly. At another point, Debbie elaborated, "I don't feel unsafe. It doesn't make me feel unsafe, because they're generally pretty cowardly people. They're not the people I fear. It comes in waves, and it's happened for so long that it doesn't have any meaning to me anymore." She minimized the attacks, saying, "It's just a minor annoyance. I don't think it matters." And at still another point she declared with a rueful laugh, "I actually think it's kind of funny now. They're going to take that much time to tell me I should die. It's like, 'Okay.' "

The women in this research deploy multiple coping strategies. Some, like Debbie, narrativize their experiences into accounts in which the abuse does not affect them, even as they behave in ways that suggest otherwise. Some respond with acts of resistance, in which they fight back and advocate change. And many try to minimize the impact of the abuse by carving out enclaves of

Credible Threat. Sarah Sobieraj, Oxford University Press (2020). © Oxford University Press.
DOI: 10.1093/oso/9780190089283.001.0001.

like-minded peers where they can find support and speak freely. All these are coping mechanisms: concrete actions taken in an attempt to mitigate the psychological harms of difficult social experiences (Pearlin and Schooler 1978).

It Doesn't Bother Me: Emotion Work as Ameliorative Labor

It is difficult to imagine such incessant toxicity *not* being upsetting. Still, people are different, so perhaps, for Debbie, rape and death threats, unsolicited pornographic images, defamatory content, and invasion of privacy are truly not upsetting. But if none of the harassment matters, if it really does not bother her, then her precautionary behaviors don't make much sense. Why reach out to the FBI, relocate your office, and walk to your car poised to call emergency service if you are not concerned or afraid? Even Debbie's small choices seem to belie her assertions. For example, she hired someone to manage her public social media accounts. Doesn't that choice suggest she found them hard to manage? At one point during our interview, Debbie said that the messages she receives privately, via email, direct messages on social media platforms, and through the post, are "much more extreme in their language and their threats and their sexism." Since she had already indicated that the public hostility did not trouble her, I asked whether these more virulent, private attacks made her uncomfortable. "No," she insisted. "I think it's really easy to scan them and then delete them. I put them in 'love mail' and 'hate mail' and then 'threats.' There are 3 different folders." If she is not troubled, why organize and save the communiqués?

As I gathered data, this puzzle resurfaced. About one-third of the women I interviewed claimed they were untroubled by the attacks they weathered, even as they shared upsetting experiences and described their tactics for avoiding, reporting, and preparing for them. While the accounts given by two participants suggest that they truly were unfazed, far more of the accounts contained discrepancies similar to Debbie's. The women assure me that the attacks rolled off their backs, yet they sought therapy for post-traumatic stress disorder (PTSD) related to online harassment, outsourced their social media management to get some distance, withdrew from unsafe spaces, and took significant security measures in their day-to-day lives.

This mismatch between the visible (and understandable) impact the identity-based abuse has had on the women I interviewed and their narratives of indestructability gave me pause. Eventually, I started to push back—gently. For Jan, the wise-cracking, lesbian pundit who, in Chapter 2, described digital toxicity as "the price of doing business," the price has been steep. When Jan makes one of her frequent television appearances, she often finds a hundred or more identity-based attacks lobbed at her on Twitter and by email. The venomous criticism includes homophobic slurs, digs at her physical appearance, and rape threats. Some of the attacks have been anti-Semitic. Early in our interview, Jan laughed about the ugliness and told me she has a "pretty thick skin." When I challenged her, asking her if what she's saying could really be true, things became clearer. She corrected course without missing a beat, "Sorry, no, of course. Of course, it matters. I don't want to undersell it. Like, I've worked very hard to not give a shit, right?"

These inconsistencies are not an indicator that Debbie, Jan, or others like them are lying to me or to themselves, They are evidence that coping is an active process. To the extent that women live peacefully in the face of identity-based attacks, in virtually every case, it is because they have labored to minimize the impact. I asked Jan what that labor looks like—what it means when she says that she has "worked very hard not to give a shit." She explained:

> I have worked hard to cultivate an attitude of shoulder-shrugging cal-lousness. Because what else am I going to do? I can't go through [life] constantly depressed. That doesn't work, that's not functional. Every time I get a hate tweet, I can't be like, "Ah, there's the downfall of civilization again." So, what's my alternative? I like what I'm doing. I believe that the collective good of my work is more important than the individual harm to me. So I've got to find a way to cope. I've been struggling with this. . . . And it's partly because I don't want to let on that it actually is—it works. It *is* frightening. On the other hand, it feels like it gives it power to admit that it does.

Other women's responses were similar, and they call to mind Arlie Hochschild's twin concepts of emotion management and emotion work, introduced to sociologists in the late 1970s. As she wrote, "By 'emotion work' I refer to the act of trying to change in degree or quality an emotion or feeling. . . . Note that 'emotion work' refers to the effort—the act of trying—and not to the outcome, which may or may not be successful" (1979, 561). Hochschild distinguished between emotion-management, which is centrally about how people *try to feel*, specifically in professional contexts, from Erving Goffman's attention to how people *try to appear as though they feel*. Jan is engaged in both types of labor: she undertakes emotion work in hopes that she will truly not care about the harassment, and, in the absence of complete success, she tries to hide the feelings she would prefer others not know she has (Goffman 1959).

Fact-checker Maria spoke pointedly about her emotion work:

> I know that we have emotional reactions, but for me, it's like I have the emotional reaction and then I think, "Is this person important? Does this person's opinion matter to me?" If the answer is no and no, I try to just go on and not let it bother me. It is hard because it's almost like an internal . . . it's trying to cultivate a certain mindset towards insults and intimidation so you can continue doing the work. . . . That sounds funny, because caring is an emotional response, but I don't think people have—Whether you care about something or not, it's not a completely involuntary decision.

She describes working to manage her emotions, and through her use of words such as "try" and "hard," it becomes clear that this is often easier said than done. Maria socializes other women into this work, as well:

> My main thing is, and I tell the women journalists that I mentor, you have to be really tough. You can't let the gendered insults, or even the general insults get to you. Sometimes, yeah, we're human. They will get to us, but we have to find a way to keep on because the insults against the media are not going away. . . . It's just not. It's gotten worse in the time I've been working as a journalist . . . on Twitter, there's a lot of gendered stuff. I'll go to [my female colleagues] and I'll say, "Are you okay?" I'll say, "Remember, you can't let these people get to you."

Thanks to Jan's candor, constructed "not caring" began to reveal itself to me in many women's stories. Billie, the broadcaster, described trying to trick herself out of caring by focusing on positive feedback: "I always try to notice how many. . . . I'm the kind of person that I can have 700 people say something nice to me, I'll remember the one bad comment someone leaves, so I try to remind myself constantly that I have so much more support than I do detraction." Here, "trying" involved reframing her experiences. Annelise, the prolific young nonprofit director, saw being visibly upset as letting her attackers "win": "I struggle with not wanting to give these people the time of day. Because a big part of it is them wanting to take your energy and drain [you], and to make you fearful." Refusing to "whine and complain" is a big part of the approach that Cheryl, the long-form journalist uses, lest she be distracted from her reporting, and Lynette, the public intellectual, works hard to hide that she cares about her abuse, a la Goffman:

> I know the game well enough to know that the only thing that the person who did it wants is to have me say how horrible it was. You can't even express it; you can't acknowledge it. There's nothing you can do, because then it just feeds that beast. It is the thing that I hate worst of all in a life that is really quite spectacularly great right now.

Although "not caring" suggests an absence of concern, most of the women who claim that they "don't care" about hostile treatment work pointedly to suppress caring as a way to cope with the attacks. This is true, even for Debbie. She let down her guard as we neared the end of our interview, acknowledging both the pain and the energy she invests to contain it. When I asked her what other people fail to understand about the harassment of women online, she sighed:

> A lot of people don't understand the potential harm. It's exhausting, and it's a low level of trauma. As someone who works in trauma, I see that and I feel it. I take measures to protect against that. I think I'm effective at doing that, but at the end of the day it's worrisome. . . . It changes your life and can change it in profoundly negative ways. I don't think people understand the effects.

Hiding the harm through narratives of resilience is not only a way to prevent the trolls from "winning" but also a crucial way that women reconcile the fear and humiliation of digital harassment with their pre-existing sense of themselves as strong, intelligent, respected, and successful. In this way, "it doesn't bother me" stories serve a second purpose. As Douglas Ezzy, building on Margaret Somers (1994), suggests, "A narrative identity provides a subjective sense of self-continuity as it symbolically integrates the events of lived experience in the plot of the story a person tells about his or her life" (1998, 239). The women in my study wanted to assert that online harassment is horrific, damaging, and needs to stop, while also rejecting the idea that they are victims or have been undone by the attackers. Their narratives of indifference and indestructibility let these two seemingly contradictory claims co-exist, by positioning the targets—themselves—as resilient and "gritty" survivors.

None of this should suggest that women are devastated by identity-based attacks online or that they are even always bothered by them. Indeed, in this research, an impact continuum emerges. The degree of harm is shaped by the severity and invasiveness of the abuse as well as the status, prestige, and security of the women under fire. It is considerably easier for a woman who lives in a safe environment, has job security, a strong reputation in her field, employment within a high-status organization or institution, and/or the financial resources to mount a lawsuit or invest in increased security to "shrug off" attempts to shame, intimidate, and discredit them. It is far harder for those struggling to get a foot in the door, working freelance or adjunct, lacking an established reputation that belies defamatory content, feeling physically unsafe in their communities already, and/or surviving on the margins, socially or financially.

Fighting Back and Pressing for Change: Resistance as Coping

Fighting back helped many of the women in this study cope with their feelings of shame, fear, and powerlessness. In the context of the prevalent "do not feed the trolls" mantra and the paucity of options for recourse via legal or platform interventions, their acts of resistance help rebuild a sense of efficacy while simultaneously working to de-incentivize and reduce digital toxicity. Women who speak out about online abuse, out attackers, attempt to create safer platforms, and work with advocacy organizations described feeling empowered by the sense that they were "doing something" rather than passively accepting the hostile climate or "opting out" of digital publics.

Women's efforts to call attention to digital toxicity and spur change came in many forms. Esther, Cheryl, Colu, Lucy, and Ivy were among those who published stories and personal essay about online abuse in prominent newspapers and magazines (indeed, these stories helped me find some of them). Others, including Jennifer, Coral, and Hazel, have given multiple public talks on the issue, while Billie, Nadine, Jan, and Fiona have appeared in videos addressing abusive digital cultures. A few women blogged about the attacks. Most, at one time or another, shared their thoughts on their social media accounts. And many of these women have been interviewed publicly about their experiences with gender-based attacks.

That this is resistance is of little doubt. Listen to Hazel, whose "death threats went mega-viral" and who subsequently participated in over 100 interviews about women's harassment online (note that I have changed some details to protect her identity):

> When they targeted me, I had one mission. . . . I was going to go over their heads and get the attention of people that could [do some-thing]. So when NBC started calling me, CNN, ABC, BBC, CBS—I was all over the world. . . . I wanted to put such a public pressure on them. Force them to recognize the severity of the attacks. . . . I just said, "The world's got to know about it."

Hazel believed the attackers wanted her to cower. Her refusal made an impact. Hazel, along with several of the other high visibility women in this research, helped thrust online harassment into mainstream news outlets and, ultimately, prompted some platforms and lawmakers to attempt to move the needle on online abuse and safety, however modestly.

The impulse to make the attacks visible, articulated so clearly by Hazel, resurfaced in another form of resistance: "outing" attackers and their vitriol. Cheryl found that much of her identity-based abuse came from men using their real names. It galled her that they were not embarrassed to behave this way, and she thought drawing public attention to their attacks might shame them out of doing the same to other women. Here she is, mid-story:

> Not only did he use his real name, but he was the head of a major organization. . . . This just was astounding to me. "Wow dude, really? You want to do that? Go ahead. I'm going to put it right up online. I will quote you accurately. Bring it on dude. Wow, this sheds a lot of light on you. Thank you for shedding light." I turned the personal [attacks] into public ones. I put them on Twitter. I didn't put every single thing on Twitter, but what I would do is say, "Ok, today I got 200 emails. Several were from this [person], several from that [one]. Here was the highlight." . . . I felt like if people were going to comment

like that, they should be exposed for commenting like that. . . . I felt, "Okay, I wrote this piece. All is fair in love and war. If you want to criticize it, that is your right, but you're not going to do it on the downlow. If you want to write me some gross sexual comment, fine. I'm going to put it on Twitter."

Lucy, the freelance science and technology journalist, also felt it was important to make public the abuse that tormented her privately.

> When I tweet about stuff that I receive, negative things . . . [i]t suddenly takes the interaction out of it being a private interaction between two people which feels very personal and very, kind of, almost shameful. Then, by publicizing that behavior and then seeing a response from normal, right-thinking human beings on the internet who are critical of it, it suddenly, for me, mitigates any kind of damage that such a personal attack could cause.

Cheryl and Lucy both value publicness, for different reasons. For Cheryl, outing her attackers is about calling them out publicly for their offensive behavior, whereas for Lucy, outing her attackers is a way to build community and reassert the bounds of social acceptability. When she publicizes the hostile treatment, people reassure Lucy that her attackers are grossly out of line. Jan uses outing in order to shift shame—to take the feelings so central to the experience of being attacked in this way and put them, instead, on those who should feel ashamed of their behavior toward her:

> I did start developing this habit of reposting the ones that I just find to be—either actually laughable or so odious. I mean, I kind of want to make fun of them at the same time, but I point out to people that this isn't fair. This is what women, especially women, especially certainly queer folks, obviously I think people of color statistically experience it worse, but this is what you have to deal with. And I don't, part of the whole point of trolling is to make you feel ashamed to speak out and I wanted to kind of defang that.

Like Hazel on the interview circuit, self-effacing Jan wants the world to know that women, especially those from underrepresented groups, are targeted by abusive identity-based attacks. Fiona, the vlogger, described the act of

sharing abusive messages publicly as a way of increasing visibility and building solidarity:

> I was getting a lot of comments that I felt like I would read them and
> I would internalize them. I felt like, if I have to see these comments,
> I want other people to have to see these comments and deal with the
> fact that this is a reality that women on the Internet face. I felt like it
> was more useful to broadcast it and make it public than have it some-
> thing that I see and delete and I'm the only one who knows about
> it. There's a solidarity in it, too, because I'll post stuff and then other
> women on the Internet will say, "I got comments like this, too. It's not
> just you who's getting it. We're all getting comments like this."

Publicizing invites social support and many women ultimately develop personal relationships with peers who can relate to the burden of digital misogyny. Unfortunately, both speaking out and "outing" attackers are often met
with additional abuse. That's why Lucy was reluctant to write about digital
sexism: "I've always shied away from writing about it, because you end up getting more hassle just by talking about it." And Esther, who works with many
women who have been attacked online, has talked about this double-edged
sword with her peers. They fear reprisal: "It's hard to talk about, because if you
write about it, it invites exactly the kind of abuse that is so worrisome." Still,
most of the women who have gone public believed the benefits outweigh the
costs. Billie faced considerable backlash when she circulated just a sample of
the abuse that had been directed at her, but she didn't regret it: "Of course the
trolls came out of the woodwork, which we knew they were going to do, but
they came out of the woodwork and I felt like I had had my say, finally, on like a
massive scale, so it didn't hurt as much as it had before." Going public with her
attacks ameliorated the harm because the subsequent outcry of disgust and
support marked her harassment as illegitimate and unacceptable, providing
validation and critical distance.

Speaking publicly about online harassment and "outing" attackers are just
two forms of resistance used by the women in this research. Some participants resisted through more traditional forms of activism, becoming involved
with or supporting advocacy organizations working on online harassment
such as the National Network to End Domestic Violence, Cyber Civil Rights
Initiative, Women's Media Center, and Online SOS. Others pressured tech
companies, including Twitter, Facebook, and Google, for change. And a few

women I interviewed collaborated with policymakers in hopes of promoting greater safety and security for women online.

Due to the considerably smaller numbers of women active in these influential circles, it is difficult to provide details of their activism and ensure their confidentiality. However, Esther, the media critic, is among the most proactive, and she has permitted me to offer some carefully redacted excerpts and summaries of her story as an example of what vigorous resistance to identity-based attacks online might involve (some key details have been omitted and minor facts changed to protect her identity). When I asked how she became so vocal on these issues, Esther described a progression of resistance that began with speaking out publicly. She received copious amounts of digital misogyny herself but told me that she reached a sort of tipping-point when she began to realize how widespread and destructive the attacks were:

> I started talking to a lot of women and what was so disturbing to me was several, in a very short amount of time, said to me, "Actually, I'm not gonna write anymore" or "I'm not gonna write about these topics that are important to me anymore. I'm worried about my own emotional well-being, my physical safety, my children." That, I thought, was, as you know, really serious. . . . Several of them sort of talked about the fact that they just "didn't want that ugliness in their lives." . . . I've heard that over and over again. . . . Then, I started writing about online harassment, but also the ways in which our mainstream norms, offline, were creating a situation online that so disadvantages girls and women.

As women's accounts of digital misogyny piled up, Esther felt overwhelmed by anger. She impulsively reached out to an executive at a major social media platform:

> One morning I was really . . . [I had heard] one [story] too much for me. It was just too much. . . . I wrote [executive's name redacted] a letter. I didn't know [this person], but I was really pissed off. I was like, "Hi. You don't know me, but I [use your platform], and this is what happens to me regularly." Also, I said, "And by the way, if I have to watch women being tortured and raped, you have to watch it, too, so here you go."

In her letter, Esther suggested several interventions the platform might make, anticipating the free speech argument against censoring even hateful speech online:

> Here [are some concrete steps your company] needs to take if you are serious about women's rights and free speech, because I keep hearing about [redacted] free speech, and what I keep seeing are suppressions of women's speech and violence toward women being tolerated [redacted] on your platform.

To her surprise, the executive responded promptly, in an affirming way, and connected Esther with an appropriate surrogate who would explore these issues with her. The delegate, however, was less meaningfully engaged. It became clear that he intended only to placate her. Frustrated and angry, Esther did what well-networked activists do: she collaborated with other activists, across organizations, to engineer a public relations campaign targeting the platform. Within days, these activists were negotiating with the platform and had gained some modest concessions. Today, Esther continues to be a leader in efforts to stop online harassment. She is deeply involved in social movement organizations and coalition work and has standing as a valued participant in conversations with tech companies, academics, and lawmakers.

Most women I spoke with are less deeply invested in large-scale resistance than Esther, but many use resistance as a coping mechanism and tool for change in some capacity. Several, including Hazel, Annelise, Maya, Ivy, and Willa, have had a meaningful impact on public awareness, social support, and reforms related to digital abuse.

Privilege and Coping

While emotion work and resistance are popular coping strategies among the women you have met throughout this book, these tools are more readily available to and effective for women who are relatively privileged. I found it interesting that most of the women I interviewed brought up, without prompting, the severity of the abuse directed at women with multiple marginalized identities. Virtually every White woman commented on the racist treatment of women of color, for example. And even though Fatima faces severe intersectional

abuse as a Muslim woman, she spoke compassionately about how upsetting it
is to see the way transwomen are treated online. Less readily visible, perhaps,
is the extent to which women's social location shapes what they perceive as
threatening and which coping mechanisms they adopt.

One of the last interviews I conducted for this project was with Jill, a
White public intellectual, author, and academic. During the interview, our
rapport was strained, and I felt a bit uncomfortable during portions of our
conversation. In hindsight, the transcript makes clear what went wrong; I was
reluctant to believe her. Jill indicated at several points, in different ways, that
the online attacks did not bother her. At times she said it outright; in other
moments it was implicit. She relished, for instance, sharing one of her "favorite" pieces of hate mail. Here she is mid-story, explaining why it didn't not
bother her:

> I see it so often online, honestly, I could read—I'll read you some-
> thing. I pulled it up, it's one of my favorite pieces of hate mail ever.
> The reason I'm going to read it to you is because it's an example of
> how not seriously these people need to be taken. . . . Oh it's great. It's
> beautiful. Beautiful piece of hate mail.

The example was a brief, obscenity-laden screed against Jill and her feminist
writing that somehow contained 10 uses of vaginal epithets, three rage-filled
references to oral sex, a couple of generic threats, and a well-worn sexist
stereotype.

Jill's sarcasm was not particularly unusual. Most women, even those traumatized by online harassment, laughed at times about the outrageousness
of the hate they encountered. This was particularly true when the rage felt
bizarrely disproportionate to the supposed transgression, was riddled with
misspellings and grammatical errors, or was unintentionally ironic (e.g., an all-
caps, exclamation point filled exhortation that the target needs to calm down).
So, humor can be a way of coping, but Jill did not seem to be struggling with
the abuse. Unlike Debbie and Jan, Jill's account did not include hints that her
"not caring" was hard-earned or carefully nurtured. She did not take extra
security precautions, outsource her social media management, or otherwise
suggest she was fearful or beleaguered. Instead, Jill seemed a picture of organic
indifference. But how, I wondered. She has been singled out on conservative
websites, even pilloried on talk radio, neither of which make for a comfortable
digital life. She helped me to understand:

I'm not interested in martyring myself. Like I will sometimes retweet people that say stupid shit to me like that, because I want the world to see what's going on, right? Like, people need to know and so I will do that. But I am not going to stand up and say, "Boo-hoo, poor me. I have to deal with idiots calling me a cunt." Like, it's not that bad. I don't know, it's not that bad. This might just be my personality, right, and it might be that I grew up working class and partly rural and, you know, I have a different idea of what hardship is, you know.

Casey, another of the White academics, had also indicated that she was unfazed by the hostility directed at her. I initially assumed this lack of concern could be traced to the less voluminous, less severe attacks she had encountered. But like Jill, Casey linked her unflappability to her class background, which she thought had lowered the bar for what might feel threatening.

You know, you grow up in a rough neighborhood or you get sexually harassed when you're young, you know. . . . [N]othing that was happening [online] was out of the ordinary or shocking to me. I don't know, maybe I'm downplaying it too much, but I'm not saying that those things aren't shitty to happen, but it actually just didn't, I don't know, it didn't really rattle me. . . . It never reached the threshold of actually bothering me. And again, that's our life trajectories, set us up in different ways to be more or less numb to those kinds of things, I think.

Social class did not come up in most of the interviews, so I have no way to explore Jill and Casey's implicit hypothesis. It is entirely possible that among the women most troubled by the harassment, there are plenty of women from lower socioeconomic backgrounds. But, if the relationship between class background and perception of threat remains unclear, the role of privilege is somewhat clearer. Jill and Casey's academic credentials, prestigious occupation, and Whiteness make it easier for them to disregard digital attacks from strangers. These markers of respectability serve as buffers, albeit penetrable ones. It is harder (though certainly not impossible) to convince an audience that Jill or Casey is a stupid, lying whore, for example, than it is to denigrate women with less perceived gravitas. Anastasia, the Black journalist and blogger, has been targeted on multiple platforms with intersectional identity-based attacks. She has been called a "nigger bitch" and "feminazi" on many occasions.

She has dealt with rape threats, references to lynching, and caustic comments about her weight. The abuse, she notes, is particularly bad when she speaks publicly about race, gender, and class inequality. When I asked whether it ever frightened her, Anastasia said no. Like Jill and Casey, she thought her class background explained her sense of physical safety:

> I grew up in the hood. I know when it's really dangerous. I know, I can sense when it's real danger. And while the online insults and the racial epithets are hurtful and they suck, most of the time, 9 times out of 10, these fools aren't going to do anything else. It doesn't go beyond that, with the exception of the guy who thought he was going to come from [redacted] and hang me, there's nothing, there's no *there* there. So, I never really feel like my safety is an issue.

But, in contrast to Jill and Casey, Anastasia *did* find the attacks threatening, if not to her physical safety. The attacks often paint an image of her as an "angry Black woman"—an insinuation made dangerous because it maps neatly onto the sapphire stereotype long deployed to discredit politically vocal Black women (Harris-Perry 2011). If outsiders believe these characterizations are credible, they undermine Anastasia's perceived integrity as a journalist, by painting her as incapable of being fair or judicious. Anastasia tries to "roll with it" and she is quick to joke about the trolls, but "not caring" is a luxury she cannot afford. This undoubtedly plays a role in why she finds the abuse emotionally taxing, such that, as mentioned earlier, she periodically changes her avatar to a photo of a White man. Whiteness and maleness, even in a tiny digital photo, serve as effective "camouflage."

For women earlier in their careers, who have yet to establish a solid body of work, professional reputation, or credibility, attacks filled with defamatory or humiliating content often feel profoundly dangerous, even if we hold race constant. Similarly, women who are in situations of economic precarity or professional instability frequently have more to lose when targeted: journalists and pundits who do freelance or independent contract work, academics who are untenured or working in adjunct or temporary positions, bloggers and vloggers dependent on advertising revenue, and those in grant- and/or donor-driven nonprofit or activist work are particularly vulnerable to attacks that strive to shame or discredit them.

These differences in status and standing—if not explicitly differences of class, race, and the like—were apparent to several of the women I interviewed.

Cheryl, for example, found the misogynistic comments directed at her disgusting and discouraging, but said she felt insulated by many of the most outrageous accusations because she had earned respect in her field. She contrasted her security with that of other women who do not yet have her professional stature:

> My main concern is about younger people, women, getting into this. Not to take it off myself, but I think I've done this long enough and I have enough of a body of work . . . that you can judge and criticize and like and whatever you want, but I clearly have been doing this and I'm not having to prove whether I can do it. I can do it. You could hate what I do, but I do it.

And listen to Ivy, who knows firsthand how different it is to be attacked as a neophyte than it is for a well-respected writer with a major national publication:

> I think one of the assumptions that I've come across . . . is that the bigger . . . a deal you are, the more people who read your stuff or know who you are, like the worse rep . . . you get. In my experience, it was worse when I was this unknown person writing for this local paper, because it felt so much more personal and . . . these people knew where I lived, knew where I worked. That was the most, I think, frightening. Also, I had no reputation. I was so [completely] lacking in confidence in my job because I had just started doing it several months before, like a year before. And so, I think, at that point . . . if [the attackers] had gone about it another way—like spreading rumors about me on the Internet or something—they would have overwhelmed my online presence, which was very small at that time. I think there's that point where you're sort of known but . . . Also, I was making like no money at the time and I was living by myself. I don't know. It was like the less established I was, the more [the online attacks] seemed like something . . . that could knock me off of whatever path . . . I was on.

Of course, in addition to having a "body of work" or an established "reputation," Cheryl and Ivy have many other markers of respectability. Signifiers such as academic credentials, Whiteness, thinness, citizenship, and well-regarded employers make it more difficult to discredit them (at least successfully). Women who lack such signifiers, even those who are similarly established, are more vulnerable to public shame and delegitimization. The vicious misogyny directed at Parker, the Latinx woman who worked on the erotic magazine, was incredibly damaging. Existing gender and ethnic stereotypes coupled with the stigma attached to women who appear to enjoy sex, supported the ugly commentary about her, lending it a manufactured air of plausibility. The ruthless indictments of her sexual behavior and morality, salacious comments about her appearance, and misogynistic jokes at her expense were far more impactful than they might have been without those long-standing cultural myths and biases. While Parker might have liked to "not care," it would have been much more challenging for her than for women who know outsiders are unlikely to give the ugly assertions much credence. So, as described briefly in Chapter 2, Parker coped by trying to escape. She withdrew socially and from her work on the magazine. She immersed herself in distractions, which proved toxic, too:

> I stopped working on the magazine. It was too depressing. It was too much. I felt like I walked out in public, and I was the scorned, the slatternly woman . . . a scarlet letter kind of experience. I know [another writer] was feeling that, too. I became very depressed. I had a shopping addiction. I was coping with it in different ways. I had a computer gaming addiction.

She cared. The abuse mattered. The volume and intensity of the attacks against Parker were more extreme than the attacks faced by Cheryl or Ivy. They were also more extreme than those aimed at some of the women who coped by working not to care, including Maria and Jan. This variation in severity likely accounts for some of the variation in both perceived threat and in preferred coping strategy. We know for example, that in cases of sexual harassment in the workplace, severity of harassment shapes if and how women respond (Lazarus and Folkman 1984; Cortina and Wasti 2005; Baker, Terpstra, and Larntz 1990). But low social power is also a predictor of who is targeted (Terpstra and Cook 1985), so disentangling severity, social location, and threat is not straightforward.

Many women who are relatively privileged are deeply upset, even traumatized, by digital toxicity, including some of the women who do emotion work intended to manage those feelings. The point here is that women who are marginalized not only receive more and qualitatively different digital pushback, but the content often feels (and *is*) more deeply threatening to them. That fact shapes how they respond to and cope with the attacks. Just as working not to care might be a harder row for them to hoe, they may find resistance riskier. Women who respond to the abuse by speaking publicly can anger attackers, something particularly unappealing if there is reason to believe that the attacks will be professionally or personally destructive. Similarly, those who choose to retweet or post examples of the abuse they face ultimately make it more visible—a desirable outcome when bringing the content to light rallies support and solidarity. But what if you are afraid the content will shape the way people see *you* rather than how they see digital culture? And not everyone is able to prompt a reply, never mind meaningful engagement, from tech companies and lawmakers when they advocate change. Would the executive have replied to Esther were she not a prominent activist and author with a national platform? It is hard to envision this as the go-to approach for people without a high-status position in a well-known organization, an array of influential social contacts, or a powerful sense of efficacy. Even Esther, a thought leader with visibility and influence, laughed about her choice to write a letter to a tech executive who had no reason to listen to her. She had been surprised to get a response. Would a less influential woman have tried to reach out? Would anyone have answered her?

Safer Spaces and Social Support

Many women cope with identity-based attacks by seeking refuge in digital enclaves. This makes sense, because despite the ubiquity of digital harassment, social support can be hard to find. Often co-workers, family, and friends simply do not understand what it is like to be targeted. Sometimes well-intentioned confidants overreact, leaving the victim to calm and console the person to whom they have turned for support. At the other end of the spectrum, sometimes outsiders are dismissive, perhaps in an effort to be reassuring, leaving the victim feeling both isolated and foolish. So even though the internet is seemingly the source of the "problem," there can be enormous relief in entering smaller spaces for conversations with other women who know how unnerving identity-based attacks can be. Gatekeeping functions such as privacy settings, password protection, and direct messaging allow enclaves to offer freedom for like-minded or similarly situated women to speak privately about the misogyny and abuse they have experienced.

Most of the women I interviewed for this research participated in and appreciated digital enclaves. Those who found the abuse particularly threatening were most likely to describe these refuges as essential. For example, gender-based attacks are especially damaging for women in heavily male-dominated fields. These women already feel as though their contributions are consciously and subconsciously minimized because they are female. As a result, speaking up about the body-centric gendered abuse (much of it sexualized) is made more difficult, because they do not want to underscore the fact that they are women. You may recall that Cat, the young sports analyst, seemed to put on armor at work (attempting to deflect criticism by using statistical methods, making hyper-vigilant accuracy checks, and wearing glasses to de-sexualize herself), but she found that fans—her audience—still saw her as "a gendered, sexualized person or object." Calling out her harassment did not feel like an option, because it red-flagged her as a woman, which could—sadly enough—be professionally damaging. She tried to leave words like "sexism" and "gender" out of the conversation, so she would be seen as a professional, not as a woman—or worse, a woman who complains. She reflected:

> It's certainly hard for me to construct my own language around this because, for almost a year, probably over a year now, I've just been talking about it in terms that are most palatable to the people whose minds I'm trying to change. That means that I cannot be as forthcoming most of the time, as I would like to be. Or as challenging to behaviors as I would like to be. It certainly comes across as a gender thing that I need to play someone who is nice and who is neutral and use this neutral language.

I pressed, asking, "If you came in and said, 'I'm dealing with this ridiculous sexism,' what is the potential risk? What might they think?"

> There is so much tone policing I'm not even sure. . . . So much of my message could get lost in how I phrase it. I've seen it happen with other women. . . . There's only so much you can do. It's just such a difficult situation to be in when you have to police almost your own feelings in order to make a broader point of social justice. As a result, sometimes I have found myself getting angry at women who are being just totally, bluntly honest about the experiences that they had, because I feel that it jeopardizes the "larger mission" of trying to get men to pay attention. . . . The impression I've had from other women [in the field] is that there's an aspect of paying your dues and staying

silent about everything until you get to a point where . . . you can't jeopardize your own position. . . . But . . . that it's considered unprofessional [to speak up]. It can be a liability to people who want to hire you, who want to collaborate with you. It's just not good.

For Cat, resistance—even speaking up—felt like professional suicide. Feeling simultaneously constrained and conspicuous made support groups particularly meaningful for her. Free from scrutiny and threat, Cat could let her guard down:

> I know quite a few of my friends who have the same philosophy as I do in terms of wanting to advocate . . . feminist ideals and inclusionary journalism and all of that; they have gone the route of having a public Twitter and then having a private Twitter, wherein you can't tell from the name on the Twitter account or the handle of the Twitter account whose it is. Then there's a little network of private Twitters, where people will share this information. Publicly, someone will respond to a terrible article about women and say, "this really isn't great." Then privately, they'll rage about it for 10 tweets: "This guy is an asshole, he does not care about women. Don't you guys remember that time 6 months ago that he also did this other terrible thing?" I think the potential to have a free voice is really great, but they need to have a safe space for it. Can't be understated. Had I not had a place where I could go and talk about the [scary messages] as they were coming in and talk about how isolated I felt. . . . All of that was so important . . . knowing that my thoughts are protected there has been essential.

Fatima was enthusiastic when she spoke about her "support groups." The enclaves she called her "Lady Army" helped her cope with digital harassment as well as the quotidian difficulties of working in a male-dominated field rife with sexism:

> I keep mentioning support groups. I have many, many. I call it my "Lady Army." [We] send cartoons and love and pictures of baby otters and just are literally lifting each other up—because you're trying to do all of this work, but then you're battling. . . . There's a group where some of the women have—Women shock me with how many

women in [this field] are survivors of sexualized violence. I had no idea. It's like 1 in 5 women in the United States have been victims of violence. But how often that can come [up through online harassment] and it can trigger—When people make these comments, they don't know what your life history is. It could be very triggering. So, these groups are so important, because when those days where I'm like, "I just don't want to do anything. I'm exhausted." And it doesn't always have to be something that is triggered by a troll. It could be that and then *plus* you had a horrible editorial meeting. Or, the piece didn't take the shape you wanted it to, or you're overwhelmed. . . . Women that are in [this field] are not in it for the money. I can really tell you that. . . . The shit that they had to wade through and navigate through to even get there is mind boggling. And, daily. Just, daily the stuff that they go through.

Grace, the investigative reporter, writes primarily about a male-dominated topic. She, too, described leaning heavily on a closed group of women working in the same field (and dealing with the same digital toxicity). Grace indicated that the participants in her Facebook group were great for commiseration but also called on each other for help managing specific instances of gendered hostility:

We need people to help us manage bad shit on social media, especially on Twitter. . . . People post the stuff they write and then they will post hate that they're getting that they want people to jump in on or just to vent. . . . Sometimes it's just, they want to be like, "Why are people like this?" But sometimes it's like, "Can you guys report this account for me?" And then it's general discussion about stuff. Like either . . . "What would you guys do if this was you and you were in my case?" Or whatever professional thing. Or it'll be a general discussion about sexism. Or something like that. You create the communities that help you in these moments, right?

As I mentioned above, the attacks Parker faced carried particular cultural force because they were supported by a scaffolding of pre-existing sexist and ethnic stereotypes. Women like Parker, without the buffer of privilege, repeatedly spoke about the importance of digital enclaves populated by similarly positioned women. Coral, a writer of Asian descent in her late 20s, has been met with years of abuse for her controversial work related to sexuality. The unrelenting attacks have included the circulation of unauthorized pornography, pointedly racialized and sexually explicit commentary, and threats against her friends and supporters. At the time her abuse began, it was long before GamerGate. Very few people, aside from victims, were paying attention to digital harassment, and Coral felt extremely isolated as her attacks accelerated. She tried to speak out, but that only magnified the abuse and its reach:

> It was a situation where, no matter how much I spoke out against it, it was the . . . The more I spoke out, the more it continued to happen. It wasn't just directed toward me at that point. It was also affecting my friends and my family and that was the thing that got really scary. I realized that I could be strong on my own, but this could ruin the professional opportunities of the people around me. . . . It's not good to have your name linked to porn and weird things when you Google yourself.

Coral wanted to fight, but had no buffer—no body of work, impressive employer, or other signifiers of respectability—to help counter the smear campaign. She worried that continuing to be vocal about the harassment would prompt more retaliation, and further increase the visibility of the humiliating attacks. Other women who were targeted provided vital support. "There was no protocol for dealing with this type of harassment. Who were we going to call? Not the cops. It was totally anonymous . . . but there was communication between me and other women doing the same work, there was strength in that camaraderie." Coral was suffering, because of the harassment and because so many seemed to believe the lies being spread about her. As she put it, "The deep sense of betrayal really comes from when your community doesn't take your side and lets the violence go unpunished." Her digital network understood. They helped her survive.

Coral and Grace and their peers built ties to sustain themselves. Some of the harassment-oriented digital enclaves described in my interviews emerged when one woman saw another being targeted and chose to reach out. Lynette, the public intellectual, made a practice of stepping in to offer reassurance:

> I do reach out to people, whenever I see somebody about to be caught up in one of these storms, I always reach out. Especially if it's a woman. Just to say, "Listen. I know what you're going through and

just so you know, you live. I'm here. You survive. I know how it feels right now, but you survive. If I can ever help, let me know." Maybe, I'm an informal welcome wagon to those who get caught up in one of these things.

Annelise found that reaching out to others was therapeutic:

> Knowing that you're not alone is always helpful. I think one of the things [harassers] try to do is to isolate you, in addition to the silencing or active intimidation. . . . I think helping other people is something that helps me. Like, helping other people when they are getting targeted, to go through and help them with their reporting and other processes. That is very helpful to me, being able to help and support other people. . . . I have a friend who was targeted with a bunch of anti-Semitic trolling, and she was just like, "I can't read another one of these. They're so toxic. But I have to report them." So I kind of came in, and it was like, "I can go into your back-end and block all of them for you," "I could help call the contacts that I have at Twitter to help you," that kind of thing. Being able to be a service to other people is something that really helps me.

Coping by connecting is an important strategy for women who have been attacked online, especially for those with less social power. In these safe environs, they can talk about the challenges they face (e.g., lack of response from law enforcement), share key information (e.g., circulating block lists of known harassers), and offer moral support and a sense of safety in numbers. These digital enclaves and troll-management mentors are evidence of women's resourcefulness. And yet, their centrality is too often a stop-gap response to the lack of institutional alternatives.

Jennifer is a White woman in her 40s who works as a science writer for a major national publication. She relates to the world as an open-minded and analytic observer. She watches closely, listens intently, and is more comfortable behind the scenes than in the spotlight. Jennifer felt suddenly and uncomfortably conspicuous when she was attacked by left-leaning trolls on Facebook. The attackers doctored images to put her in suggestive clothing, speculated that she was involved in sexual improprieties that called her reporting into question, and used gendered epithets in an effort to discredit her. Jennifer took great comfort in speaking with other writers who had been attacked online.

These interactions were valuable in part because Jennifer didn't know what else could be done. Her editor dismissed the harassment, telling her to laugh it off, which Jennifer found a disappointing "institutional response." Still, she did not want to take it further and call even more attention to herself or to the embarrassing accusations and images. Women in male-dominated fields like hers already feel conspicuous, and the body-based nature of the abuse forces their bodies, sexual behavior, and gender into the foreground. Since Jennifer's harassment subsided fairly quickly, she did not think it necessary to involve the police or seek counseling, yet it left her unsettled. Like others who found their options for formal redress lacking (see Chapter 2), Jennifer found solace in talking with other women who had "been there."

In the Wake

In sum, women targeted with digital abuse use a variety of coping strategies, such as working not to care, fighting back (broadly defined), and seeking comfort in digital enclaves. The perceived threat and real impact of online attacks are shaped by their severity and the social position of the person under attack, as well as by the extent to which the venom is supported by pre-existing stereotypes and cultural biases. More privileged women have a wider array of coping strategies available to them. Their social class; professional standing; membership in historically valued racial, ethnic, and religious groups; and possession of arbitrary markers of respectability (e.g., thinness and emotional restraint) help deflect some of the most common attacks and, in so doing, create space for speaking out and cultivated (and actual) non-caring that is less accessible and effective for women without these advantages. Privilege also increases the likelihood that these strategies will be effective. Remember, for example, the way resistance backfired for Coral but opened doors for Esther. Digital enclaves remain a critical refuge for the women for whom the attacks are most destructive. Regardless of how women cope with digital toxicity, these efforts are work. They take time. They sap energy. And they come with personal and social costs of their own.

5

Personal Troubles and Public Issues

In spite of their efforts to avoid attack and cope when targeted, the women I interviewed suffered—economically, professionally, psychologically, and socially. The toll is intensely personal for those caught in the crosshairs, but this patterned hostility reverberates, helping to sustain existing social inequalities and generating democratic disturbances that harm us all.

The Personal Costs of Identity-Based Attacks

Left with inadequate recourse and faced with unreasonable "solutions," such as moving offline or not feeding the trolls, the price of abuse is hefty. I attempt to make these individual costs clear here, both to honor the experiences of the women who shared their stories with me and to illuminate the way seemingly personal struggles ultimately amount to public issues.

THE TOXICITY TAX

Facing ongoing identity-based attacks online comes with a hefty "toxicity tax." Coral, Lynette, and Cat, for example, hired private investigators, while Maya and Lynette hired attorneys. Diana commissioned a privacy protection service to extract personal information from data brokers' websites. Ivy missed work on three different occasions so that she could appear in court to secure a restraining order. Many women's invested time and money into therapy, and some paid to outsource the management of their social media accounts. Hazel, for example, hired someone to comb through her comments and direct messages on social media, scrub her timelines of upsetting content, and post on her behalf. Still other women enlisted peers, friends, or family members to

Credible Threat. Sarah Sobieraj, Oxford University Press (2020). © Oxford University Press.
DOI: 10.1093/oso/9780190089283.001.0001.

undertake this work. The abuse against Coral targeted her loved ones so persistently that ultimately someone close to her hired a costly reputation defense company to mitigate the professional damage. Fatima ran down a lengthy list of steps she took to be—or at least, try to be—safe. Some of the efforts were costly:

> I do all of these things because I think it's important to protect myself. I take precautions when I travel. If I travel to a city I don't know, particularly in the current political climate, I'll ask for a car service—I'm not taking a cab. I want there to be someone to pick me up when I get there for safety reasons. . . . [T]his threat of [physical violence] is always pending for women. And it sucks to be working like this, but people have been very lackadaisical with online abuse because they're like, "Oh, it's not real, it's online." Oh, it's very, very real. It's very real. And I can tell you that it occupies more brain space in women than it should because it's one more thing we have to deal with. It sucks.

Fatima's "brain space" is absorbed by concern about the places she opts to stay, the potential for unauthorized surveillance, finding safe transportation, and on and on and on. Allaying her fear is worth the hassle, but staying safe is expensive, especially for a freelance writer whose income is inconsistent.

Adding insult to injury, managing digital abuse came with indirect economic costs, too. The abuse complicated women's experiences in the job market and restructured their professional opportunities. Several women worried about their ability to find employment in light of the defamatory and offensive content attackers had posted about them. Others worried whether employers would find them at all after the care they took with publicly available information. Diana, for example, was leery of LinkedIn and had one interviewer note that her profile was the most bare-bones he had seen. She found herself explaining that she had an anonymous stalker, something she would have much preferred not to discuss in a job interview.

It can be hard to know whether women lost job opportunities because hiring personnel googled them and came across defamatory content or talk of controversy. In Parker's case, there was no such mystery. Devastating abuse led Parker to work abroad for a couple of years, hoping that a change of scenery and some physical distance would help her feel safe again and get a fresh start. It seemed to work; she returned to the United States for graduate school, earned her degree, and secured a full-time position. Things were on the right track. But then, in a stunning turn of events, Parker was fired:

> I get a call from the [leader of the organization]. "We need you to come in immediately." I say, "What is this about?" and they're like, "We have some concerns about the resume, now. You need to drive down immediately." I drive down. I'm shaking. I was like, "What do you mean concerns about my resume?" The guy snarled at me. He was angry at me. . . . I remember I was shaking like a leaf the entire time. He brought in—he had different people at the meeting. I think for legal reasons. There was a woman. There was a man and a woman also in the meeting. The man was [another leader], and the woman was their technology coordinator. The technology coordinator had a paper, and [the boss] just shows me the paper. On the paper is a list of different websites about me. . . . He said, "I think you're incredibly stupid and foolish." I was so shocked, I had no idea how to even . . . I didn't even know what to say. I was just like, I couldn't believe it was happening that I was losing a job because there were crazy things about me online. . . . I didn't even have a chance to speak for—They didn't even say, "Hey, there's some stuff about you online, what do you have to say about that?"

The list of websites to which Parker is referring included misogynistic posts put up years earlier by strangers, including a persistent harasser. Exasperated, Parker marveled: "What's weird about it is that it's just garbage. None of it even makes any sense. It's just 'so-and-so is a slut, so-and-so is a whore, so-and-so is bad. I want to fuck so-and-so. So-and-so should get raped.' This stuff is making employers not want to hire people?" The head of the organization gave Parker an official letter attributing her termination to undisclosed information on her resume, as if she had done something unseemly or lied about her qualifications. Parker said that in retrospect she probably should have filed a lawsuit, but her visceral aversion to anything having to do with those memories and the shame that accompanied them got in the way.

There are, of course, myriad, smaller ways the abuse can become a financial liability. Fearing that online abuse could become physical violence, an understandable worry in light of the ubiquitous rape and death threats, Debbie, for example, said, "I don't advertise my talks. I advertise them after the fact. I don't tell people where I am. . . . That has a very detrimental effect on my ability to sell books or get people to the talk. It does inhibit me professionally, because I can't tell people when I'm going to be in their city." Lynette was similarly cautious:

> I used to have a calendar on my website, that I'm going to be at this conference or do this talk, because this is what you do. You can meet people that you have something in common with and you have a coffee. I don't have a calendar anymore. I don't know if the [attackers are] serious every once in a while when they say they want to blow my brains out or they want to kick my ass.

And, although Lynette had received several invitations to make national television appearances, she declined many of them: "People think I'm crazy because, in our world [academia], people would kill to do it. I'm like, 'Oh, hell no.' I said no so fast, I think I even shocked the bookers, because they don't get a lot of nos, I don't think. I said, 'Nope. Sorry.'" Hazel told me she had missed important professional opportunities, such as attending conventions, because of credible death threats. Visible opportunities like the ones these women turned down help to sell books, increase standing, and open other doors. Turning down moments in the limelight because of the potential for abuse and harm is an expensive and often necessary way for these public women to mitigate harm.

Reputational Harm and Professional Standing

Most professional harm comes with related economic costs, of course, but the professional toll of identity-based abuse extends beyond the economic. Established women often remain employed and employable in spite of the attacks waged against them while still wrangling with reputational harm. Reputational damage shapes the way the targets are perceived and treated by others as well as the way they feel about themselves. One pronounced fear that came up in my interviews was that the abuse—either its upsetting substance or the notoriety surrounding its volume and brutality—could overshadow women's other attributes, experiences, skills, and identities. If Parker's experience is any indication, their fears may be warranted.

The threat is especially high for young women attempting to get their careers off the ground and/or for those who may already be at the margins by virtue of their race, national origin, etc. Yet even relatively privileged women find online abuse can degrade their reputation. Billie, who is White and well-established, found the controversy surrounding her attacks had come to define her professionally:

> The fact that I [have credentials and experience], the fact that I'm very much innocent until proven guilty, none of that stuff matters, and I think that it has harmed my career. . . . [T]his [hostility] just goes on and on and on and on and you know, you feel like no matter how much you fight back against it, because this has become the narrative on Twitter, this is now what defines my career. . . . You know, there was a story written about me in [a prominent newspaper] that called me [controversial]. There's people I know who in the industry who have been like, "Oh, yeah, well . . . [because of the 'controversy'], they can't hire you," that kind of stuff, all over something that was never said.

Billie's resistance to the unrelenting attacks against her had been recast as scandal and marked her as a loose cannon, damaging her professional appeal, even though neither are fair nor accurate assessments of what transpired. The stain of harassment may bring her related speaking opportunities, but those are a double-edged sword since being associated with the "controversy" limits her long-term professional and economic potential.

Several women expressed anxiety as they watched hostile strangers attempt to discredit or humiliate them, undermining their professional credibility. One attacker made YouTube videos about Rina. They challenged the veracity of her research by painting her as an ideologue and a key figure in an elaborate feminist conspiracy. In contrast, Lucy felt she was demeaned by attacks that sexualized her and fixated on her physical appearance rather than her work. She said, "I just find that really insulting. I was on [the television program] to talk about a sort of thing which I felt was important . . . and that sort of undermines what you are saying." Whether the comments were cruel or ostensibly flattering, Lucy felt they degraded her among her colleagues.

When reputational harm is the explicit intent, attackers often deface women's likenesses, editing them into humiliating photos (often pornographic or violent), as mentioned in the Introduction and Chapter 1. Hazel found this tactic particularly horrifying:

I can't [even look at the images], because it just tears me apart so much, but they do it every day. They Photoshop me into terrible situations, sexual situations, like—you name it. You name anything, they can do it. Like they tried destroying my business. They've gone after me professionally. I had [a close relative] asking me about lies said about me, because that's how much [the attackers have] worked to savage my reputation.

Whether or not such humiliating attacks actually impacted women's reputations or damaged their economic lives, they made women feel stigmatized and uncomfortably conspicuous, shaping their professional confidence, expectations, and productivity.

LOST TIME AND PRODUCTIVITY

Hours and days are lost weeding through comments, tweets, and messages. Many women invested time documenting the abuse. They organized screen shots, printed and filed materials, and otherwise worked to create a paper trail at the request of law enforcement or employers—or simply to have evidence on hand in the event of escalation. Going to court, filing reports, blocking and reporting—all these strategies sap time. Even the emotional work is time-consuming: explaining the situation to co-workers and loved ones, participating in therapy sessions, spending time feeling upset or worried, and the like eat away at victims' days. This impacts women's personal lives, but most of the women in this study focused on how the abuse they received in the context of their professional lives took time away from other priorities. Fatima raised this issue:

I get annoyed at the amount of time it takes for me to weed through [the comments]. . . . Because I use Twitter as a tool for my career. People contact me. It would be very truthful for me to say that I have gotten a lot of work [from] meeting people through Twitter. Absolutely. Absolutely. So, I use it as a tool. And for me to have to go through my mentions and read hundreds of mentions of, "Get the fuck out of America, you don't belong here, we don't want your kind, why are you writing about [this topic]? You're stupid. Where you come from people don't even drive." . . . I get annoyed because it's time-consuming and it's exhausting. Sometimes there's those messages that are a punch in the gut. The porn thing was a punch in the gut for me. Because I'm like, "Are you serious? I just wrote about this [important event], and you're giving me hijab porn?" I was annoyed . . . because I don't think this needs to be part of the career. Because women I know spend, daily, two to three hours of their work time handling comments.

With resignation, Fatima said this was her experience, "Every day."

The time required to deal with the toxic feedback impacted many women's focus and ability to produce quality work. Kimberly described how hostile responses to one story pulled her away from reporting on the next:

I was writing about a candidate [and his alleged illegal activities]. He mobilized a lot of his supporters to go over the comments [on her story] and respond to them. . . . For my mental space, like I need to stand by my work and walk away unless there's something that someone thinks is terribly wrong, but usually it's just noise . . . and it just— it takes my energy away from where it needs to be. If I'm spending a lifetime reacting to what happened in all the stories and I'm not looking for what's going on next, I'm not in tune with what's happening [on her beat].

Several women echoed these feelings, including Billie, who bubbled over with frustration:

If someone was following me around all day on the street saying this stuff to me, they would be in jail for stalking, for harassment, for disorderly conduct, for any number of different things. But for some reason the fact that people can say it to you online where you cannot get away from it, you can't go into your house and close the door, you can't call the police, it never ends, it's 24 hours a day, but it has the same effect on you I think, where you fear for your physical safety, where you fear for your reputation, it has—Every year we get those stories about how the NCAA [basketball] tournament takes away so many hours of productivity from workplaces, this [digital toxicity] has got to be taking away a ton of time from women's productivity in the workplace, because you have to spend so much time dealing with it.

The involuntary overtime consumed by managing the influx of abusive content drains women's energy, erodes their morale, and cuts into the resources they can devote to the work they want and need to do.

Aubrey is one of the women who experimented with using male avatars as a way to temporarily escape the hostility. When I asked how she thought life online would differ if she were a man, her first response was that she would get a lot more accomplished. She explained:

> I don't actually know what it's like to be a man online, but just pretending to be one for a week was crazy. What a different experience it was. . . . [I]t was just so much less exhausting, I think that's the main thing, and you just realize how much more energy it takes to be female in an online space and what is that energy being taken away from? What other things could I be doing with that energy besides battling or dismissing all this stuff?
>
> There's a physical component to this, like you have to, each time, you have to delete the emails, you have to mute and block the account and report the scary stuff, you know, double-check all of your password things, it actually takes time out of your day. And the time to sort through the things and in order to participate because these are multiple major venues for conversation, for talking about social media, so in order to participate in that conversation, you need to [go through all the feedback to] see that another journalist has said something to you or talked about you in a positive way, or challenged your idea in a constructive way or whatever it is. In order to participate [professionally], you have to wade through all this filth and it just takes time, just literally—it takes longer for women to just do the basic function of participating, and that's even when you take out fear for one's safety, or the psychological effects that it might have on you, or the stress that it causes, and what that might do to your body, and how you might need to rest up more. It's just harder, and I don't think that people really appreciate that.

Digital misogyny generates an abundance of profoundly unpleasant, unpaid work, which comes with concomitant diffuse psychological, emotional, and physical ramifications. Together, these shape women's professional vitality and economic outcomes in addition to their overall well-being.

STRUGGLES WITH EMOTIONAL AND MENTAL HEALTH

Other than Jill and Casey (see Chapter 4), the women I interviewed described the experience of online abuse as draining and distressing. I did not ask about emotional or mental health, but these issues emerged in nearly every interview. Many people used the word "trauma" or "traumatic" in reference to the attacks. Several referred to getting professional help and/or referenced concrete diagnoses, such as depression, anxiety, or post-traumatic stress disorder. And a couple of the women described themselves as developing addictions as a result of the abuse, as we saw with Parker in Chapter 4.

Jan, the pundit, found the ugly attacks became detrimental to her well-being overall. She explained, "I was depressed. Like, I was definitely drinking a little too much, and moody, and upset, and unhappy. It sucked. It just sucked." Eventually, on the recommendation of a co-worker, Jan found some relief when she engaged less with the comments and social media posts. The difference was noticeable:

> It didn't occur to me to stop reading it, right? Like, duh. I'm such a polite person, I just read it all. So you know I had to still like make an effort to find the death threats. You had to find those and report those. But at the kind of, I wasn't poring through it in the way I kind of had been. That helped.

Jan laughed at her own earnestness and the way she felt obligated to engage with any feedback that came her way, but it bears repeating: engaging with the abusive content had deleterious effects on her mental and emotional health.

The damage is even more pronounced for those who experienced prolonged, invasive, extensive, and/or more vitriolic treatment. Diana, the businesswoman and former blogger, felt there were few people who could appreciate the multifaceted ways harassment impacted her:

> [The harassment and abuse] definitely changed, really, fundamentally changed who I am and how I relate to the world. In the worst period . . . I would have panic attacks. I was diagnosed with anxiety and depression. Even now, my therapist says I have PTSD, which, it's not really like PTSD, it's like TSD. . . . Trauma isn't something that happens to your body. . . . Fundamentally, it's a loss of trust in the world and a shift in your perspective and your way of relating to people. It's a loss of a worldview and a sense of safety. That, very much, is something that has happened to me and that I can relate to.

Diana is not the only woman in my study who carried such a burden. Coral, the blogger, recalled:

> I lost a lot of enthusiasm for life. All the things that used to bring me joy no longer did. I spent a lot of time at home. People would come over all the time. I was, like, always very extroverted and social so I don't think I ever felt like . . . There's symptoms you read about when someone has PTSD, self-isolating. I didn't really . . . It didn't seem like I was outwardly exhibiting it, but when I look back on it now—and I've done a lot of reflection on that time—it was obvious that I was not well.
>
> It literally drove me crazy. You could write that in your book. . . . I think I'm a very psychologically strong person. I've always been a survivor, but I got to a point even after I [relocated and changed my name] . . . I had a nervous breakdown, where I literally thought there were people after me and not just after me, after a whole group of women. . . . I was convinced. . . . This was my thinking and it seemed very rational at the time. . . . I've looked up my symptoms. I'm like, "Okay I suffer from persecutory delusion, learned helplessness, anxiety, imposter syndrome." I have some form of PTSD along with depression that was never really treated.

Coral is still struggling. These are deeply intimate experiences, yet, even these most personal of troubles must be re-understood as public issues. As I transition to the broader, societal-level costs of identity-based attacks online, it is instructive to listen closely to Colu, a freelance journalist, as she talks about the way her mental and emotional well-being shape the way she feels about writing:

> That's, kind of, what disquiets me most . . . there was obviously, definitely, without a shadow of a doubt, an emotional impact. I would say I felt a really—the toll on my mental health was pronounced just from—just being consistently gaslighted for a period of a few months. That toll on my mental health was horrible, and I felt really awful about myself. . . . [Y]ou almost feel a sense of just paranoia about operating in online spaces, and saying things because you realize that you're kind of in the system that is not out for your success. . . . Like, just the torrent of abuse that is possible if you say the wrong thing, or

if you speak on an issue on something like [race]. So, subsequently we had a [tv] show where there were allegations of racism. . . . And I went to an interview . . . I got the anxiety attack afterwards and just being like, you know what, I can't . . . I don't want to go back to what it was before, where it was that trauma of abuse again. So, it's like, there's the abuse, and that was that one thing, but the negative impact will stay with me, and that will mean that some things, perhaps, will just never get said. If that makes sense? I think abuse, honestly, can have a self-silencing affect because . . . it can be like, oh, I'm just not going to say that. I'm just not going to engage in that debate. I'm just going to try and be quieter. . . . So, I think, that the abuse in itself is a horrible thing, but I think its impacts afterwards are also very damaging just for freedom of expression and speech, those things.

Colu's experience with and awareness of the hostile speaking environment constrained her willingness to participate, or at least to participate in the way she might otherwise. This matters, not only because Colu's voice may be lost but also because so many others remain unheard.

Broader Costs: Identity-Based Attacks and Democratic Disturbances

Digital harassment and abuse create broad, societal-level problems that extend far beyond the individuals directly threatened by the attacks. In this section I address three distinct democratic disturbances created by the prevalence of identity-based attacks online: the patterned deterioration of political discourse, the damage to the robustness of our pool of candidates willing to run for public office (and the ability for elected officials from underrepresented groups to do their work effectively once in office), and the circulation of disinformation that interferes with election integrity and undermines the role of journalism in a healthy democracy.

WATCHING WOMEN RECEDE FROM POLITICAL DISCOURSE

Few would argue that democratic discourse is at its healthiest. Many Western democracies are plagued by polarization, animosity, and distrust, and while the United States is perhaps most infamous in this regard, many other political cultures are equally if not even more antagonistic. Switzerland, Ireland, Spain, France, Canada, Israel, Greece, Hungary, Turkey, and others are facing similar struggles (Gidron, Adams, and Horne 2019; Iyengar and Westwood 2015; McCoy, Rahman, and Somer 2018; Robison and Moskowitz 2019; Iyengar et al. 2019). What's more, voices of those from non-dominant political parties are largely overlooked (Shepard 2011); people have become more distrustful of journalism (Brenan 2019; Fenton 2019; Newman and Fletcher 2017), and too often we find our political knowledge clouded by disinformation (Bennett and Livingston 2018; Tucker et al. 2018; Wardle and Derakhshan 2017). The hostile speaking environment described in this book further undermines the robustness of public political talk by making those whose voices are already underrepresented feel more guarded and less open to joining key conversations about current affairs and the common good.

In spite of their interest in and commitment to participation, women who have experienced or witnessed identity-based attacks sometimes self-censor, refrain from dialogue, take breaks from writing or from the platforms that have proven to be the most dangerous, and, in the most extreme cases, "opt out" of public political discussions altogether.

Self-Censorship
Self-censorship was rampant among the women who shared their stories with me. Some avoided writing or speaking publicly about "high-risk" subjects. Others waded into the shark-infested waters cautiously, tempering their ideas and arguments so they would feel less dangerous. And still others stayed on safer shores and watched conversations unfold, even when they wanted to participate.

Billie, the broadcaster, is bold, defiant, angry, and strong. But the abuse targeting her made her police her own tone nonetheless, especially when it came to talking about gender issues. She said, "I really think before I weigh in on something, and I try to craft my tweets in a way that are maybe not as edgy as I normally would just because I know what's coming anytime I say anything about domestic violence or sexual assault. . . . [I]t's a pretty effective way for a certain portion of the Internet to have silenced women on a lot of issues." Time and again, Billie noted that she would be punished for addressing the subjects about which she felt most passionate. As prominent men served up misogynistic commentary that Billie felt compelled to challenge, she worried over the wrath of their fans and stopped calling them out:

> I think that for a lot of women it leads to self-censorship. So, you know that if you talk about the hot button issues, domestic violence, sexual assault, racism, misogyny, that you're going to get it, so a lot of women just don't comment on it—and there's so few women in this industry already, we really need those voices. There's certain things that I won't say. Like, I will not talk about [names two polarizing media personalities with large followings], no matter what egregious thing they say about women that week, because anytime you say anything to them or try to stand up to them, they flood you with 5,000 guys screaming at you about how terrible you are. They've managed to pretty much silence [all of us], because everyone is afraid of them and what they unleash on everyone. That's really frustrating—watching them be mainstreamed when they [produce misogynistic content], but you can't say anything back because you get killed.

Billie has not left the public eye, but the hostile speaking environment has taught her to tread carefully because some dialogues come with too steep a cost.

Rina had her own list of taboo topics: "It makes me not want to write about certain things," she sighed. She wants to protect herself, but the decision is fraught for her. I could hear Rina's frustration in her repeated allusions to the unreasonable burdens of participation. Listen to the way she struggles with this over the course of our interview:

> "At a certain point I was like, 'I'm done writing about this.' That said, I just recently made the mistake of doing it again. I was full of regret. I really was."

> "At that point, I'm like, 'No. I'm not doing it again.' I really am not interested in being attacked like that. I'm not interested in any of it."

> "The whole thing gave me pause of like, 'What am I even doing? Why would I touch that again?'"

> "I think that it makes people think twice about what it is that they write and what it is that they want to publish. This last experience

made me really sort of have that tough-love conversation with myself, where I was like, 'You gained nothing from this.' "

In the end, Rina decided to step back. Grace described a similar calculus:

> There are times where I think, "I cannot handle this today." So, on the social media front where everything's moving quickly there are times where I'm like, "Okay, I'm not going to comment on this story today, because I don't want to deal with it." Like, the return on this investment on putting myself out there on this will not be worth it.

In particular, Grace told me that participating in exchanges related to race or gender (especially sexual violence) required a willingness to deal with toxic screeds. She had become "very careful" in assessing whether she was up to participating and had grown vigilant about what to say and how to speak, in an effort to contain the blow-back.

Some insisted they would never be silenced, even as they made clear that the threat of abuse constrains them. Debbie, for example, shared some critical thoughts about a recent magazine profile about a trans celebrity, qualifying:

> I would never post that online, because I would be piled on by the left and I would be piled on by the right. Any time I post something—it's not that I shy away from specific topics. There might be certain arguments I won't make about specific topics because of the silencing identity politics on the left and the racism and hatred and misogyny on the right. Beyond specific topics, I'll look at something [I might want to say online] and I'll say, "No, this is just going to go down this nasty rabbit hole. I'm not even going to post it." It's changed my posting patterns, blocking patterns, and engagement.

Debbie speaks out regularly about issues of social and political import, but there are limits to what she will say.

Casey did not have a list of off-limit topics. Instead, she mitigated the risk of backlash by writing in ways that suggested neutrality, open-mindedness, and palatability. This style is common in academic writing, and there is nothing wrong with it. But it is significant that Casey refrained from writing in ways that were political or polemical, because she worried about the fallout:

> I would like to think [the choice to write in this way is] judicious. That's probably an overly—I don't want to give myself too much generosity in that. . . . That's a tactic that I struggle with, but it's one I'm pursuing for now. . . . There are other strategies you can take to fight those fights, and I'm not always . . . sometimes I would like to write the raging editorials but I don't because, for whatever reasons, this is the path I have—for now it's the one I use. Does that make sense? . . . The irony is my heart is with the other approach. It's always a little bit of a—and this may not be the most effective way and I don't know, I'm glad that there's other people who are kind of burning it down.

However Casey explained her style of writing to herself in the past, during our conversation it seemed the explanation felt less comfortable. She was generous to share her uneasiness so candidly. Other women described their versions of this sort of "judiciousness." Jan, for example:

> I'd be lying if I said [the potential for backlash] didn't occur to me [when I write]. I'd be lying if I said that it didn't, you know, that there wasn't a sort of portion of my brain that isn't thinking about how they're related. . . . So, like, if I'm going to say this in this way and it's going to trigger people in that way, is there a way that I could say it in an equally effective way that's less triggering?

Jan's equivocating would be unremarkable were it done to enhance clarity, mobilize interest, or maximize rhetorical force. Instead, many, like Jan, temper their opinions, insights, and arguments because they are afraid.

If some women self-censor by avoiding certain topics or via jettisoning more direct or emphatic styles of communication, others opt to sit out the discussions or speak only in safer spaces. Naomi, the undergraduate computer science major, asserted her willingness to keep talking about LGBTQ issues, but a close read reveals that she does so only when she feels safe:

> Except for these isolated incidents where other Tumblr users or like people from Reddit have come in and harassed me and my

friends, [her Tumblr is] mostly like a safe bubble, so I don't feel I have to dampen my voice, because I think most of the people listening want to hear what I have to say. I'm not in a position where I have constant harassers listening in, looking to argue with me, to give backlash. On the other hand, looking at the YouTube comments, I watch videos all the time and I think, "Man, I would have something good to say, but I don't want to have people come and say, 'Suck my dick' as a reply to an insightful and influential comment." I don't want to deal with that. It's not fun for me. So, often times even if I see something on Facebook or YouTube, I'll go back to Tumblr to post about it, because I don't really feel like getting into an argument with someone right now. I don't feel like getting harassed in those other places. Thankfully for me, Tumblr has been a space that has allowed me to not be quiet about these issues. I respect and understand and could imagine myself having to quiet down if this were constant harassment, if this were happening all the time. I don't want this to come off as saying, "Oh everyone should be vocal. It's fine, you shouldn't have to be quiet about it," because it's emotionally, physically, mentally, and economically draining to deal with harassment day in and day out. I think it's absolutely a reasonable response to step away, and I don't want to ignore that reality. But since I have not had ongoing, daily harassment, you know, my voice is not quieting down. I'm going to keep talking about these issues as long as I have the emotional and mental capacity to speak about them.

It should not be taken as a criticism of Naomi to note that she is only willing to speak up when she is surrounded by like-minded people. Instead, it should be read as a referendum on the abundant hostility that has driven so many women away from the kinds of cross-cutting political conversations that research shows are important for political engagement more broadly (Mutz 2002b; 2002a). Like Naomi, Scarlett—the game designer and professor—still speaks publicly on issues that concern her, but she does so selectively and discreetly:

I've been working on a data-driven project with a colleague that touches on [sensitive content] and we've been, even though both of us normally are inclined to publish in places that the access is open, I think we're probably not going to for that. We talked to a couple journals about if they'll let you use pseudonyms to publish peer-reviewed articles. . . . I stay out of things. I don't necessarily hashtag things. I'm careful in certain ways.

Scarlett is walking a tightrope, attempting to be visible enough to influence the conversation but private enough to avoid becoming a target. For her, self-censorship is not staying silent; it is hiding in plain sight.

The End of Interaction?

The early internet provided lay users easy access to a wealth of information, while web 2.0 ushered in interactive dynamism. The decentralization of publishing via developments such as WYSIWYG editing (which allowed everyday people to publish without needing to know how to code) and low- to no-cost user-generated content platforms democratized participation and content production. Collaborative and interactive tools such as open source software, wikis, blog communities nurtured by RSS (really simple syndication), peer-to-peer file sharing, commenting, and social gaming facilitated involvement rather than consumption only (Shirky 2008). These tools revolutionized the meaning of the internet in our lives, making it a rich and valuable way to share our ideas and connect with others. These attributes—the ability to gather, share, exchange, and respond—created digital publics. But now, it seems that many of the women in this research are retreating to older modes of internet use.

Returning to one-way, broadcast-only communication and/or reception-only consumption allows some women to avoid abuse. Many women I spoke with had disabled comments on their content. Scarlett, for example, shut down comments on select YouTube videos after being targeted. When the thwarted attackers began to comment elsewhere on her channel, she closed all commenting. Other women did their best to ignore comments. Most journalists were particularly reluctant to even look at the comments on their work, never mind engage with readers. Fatima, for example, emphasized:

> I never, ever, ever read the comments on articles that I write. Because they're garbage. They're just garbage. . . . Comments are just a cesspool of anger and hatred. They're just . . . I don't even entertain . . . Nope. Absolutely not. Absolutely will never look.

Sophia called it a "mental health exercise":

I think that, as a mental health exercise for reporters, they can't be reading readers' comments, unless you . . . Even, places like the wire services and *Wall Street Journal*, I mean, you'll just read the craziest stuff. It's a lot more highbrow than on Yahoo News, or something, but it's just, it would be an exercise in just wanting to hate, and hating humanity every day, if you did that as a reporter.

The tenor of the "feedback" drove Sophia away, she continued: "It was everything from [my] appearance, to [guessing my] potential ethnicity, to what a dumb bitch I look like, to whatever . . . people are straight up abusive. You can't read it, because you'll lose your mind."

I heard similar sentiments from women who were not working journalists and reporters. Lynette, the public intellectual, had sworn off reading comments on her work, too:

I've not read a comment on anything I've written in at least two, two and a half years. I will not search myself on the Internet, I do not want to know. When you talk about your professional life and what that means, it means I can't always pull the stuff that might be helpful, for example, for my tenure case or something like that, I'm just not going to Google my fucking name.

This is probably sound decision making on Lynette's part, but it is a choice with consequences for her and for the robustness of our public discourse. Lynette's strategy means she misses some of the ways people engage with her work, such as citations that appear in nontraditional venues and references to her scholarship in the news. She, like Scarlett, Fatima, and Sophia, misses the opportunity to communicate with laypeople who engage with her ideas, to defend or further explicate her thinking when readers proffer questions or critique, or to identify areas for growth. That loss is, of course, shared by readers interested in engaging with her and by those who may not comment but who would have appreciated following the dialogues between her and her readers.

Avoiding comments was not the only way I found women shrinking their circle of interaction. Alex, for example, loves to strike up conversations via social media, but even she changed behavior:

I stopped replying to threads. Right? Because I realized that like, "Okay, there's a weird tacit understanding that if you go online, and you reply to some bonkers thing that Alex Jones has said, now you're in their house." You've entered. So, I just stopped, because I did feel like "I'm not changing minds. Nothing good is happening. This is not useful. This is not constructive. I need to get out." So I did.

Alex wouldn't engage because she did not want to be seen as "fair game" for harassment and threats. Liz, too, had curtailed her commenting, becoming a reader rather than a discussant, as she had been in the past. This is a significant departure for Liz, who had been happily enmeshed in a network of bloggers with shared interests, in which commenting and receiving comments provided meaningful exchange and connection. Through blogging and commenting, Liz built relationships and discussed social and cultural issues. Digital hate squelched much of the pleasure she found in online life and led her to pull back. Should the threat of abuse disappear, she speculated,

> I would comment a lot more on things. . . . I would comment on a different variety of things. I would probably comment more on video games, you know? That's a thing that I really like and I never write about because it's such a male-dominated space and such an aggressive space. So even when I was writing about all these other pop culture things, [I] never wrote about video games. Whether I was playing them or not. . . . I used to comment on things a lot more, but that was years ago, before you had people like Anita Sarkeesian getting all of this blow-back, or Lindy West, or a host of other female content creators that I love and really respect getting just horribly harassed and threatened online.

On its own, Liz's unwillingness to make comments about video games may seem trivial, but the patterns matter. If women lose the opportunity to engage and readers/viewers lose the chance to talk with them, we inadvertently cede one of the greatest gifts of new internet and communications technologies.

Taking Breaks and "Opting" Out

Many women take digital breaks to escape the toxicity. Maya "went private" on Facebook and Instagram during the peak of the attacks against her. Social media breaks help her get away from the abusive responses to her work on civil rights and sexual assault, though she still thinks about leaving the public eye:

> I think about [going private] often. I don't think that anyone deserves this type of harassment, but for me personally, it's been important to feel and acknowledge that I'm making a choice to be in the public eye, and I'm making a choice to be online as me [as opposed to using a pseudonym]. It's helpful because I know that I could pull the plug any second. Sometimes I will just start ghosting social media and not post or interact or anything for a couple weeks, because I need a break.

The periodic hiatuses help her refocus on the reasons her voice matters. Maya knows her activism is important, and she values the connections she makes with women who find her openness validating. For now, those benefits outweigh the considerable burdens of participation.

Fiona also takes frequent mini-breaks. She recalled days when she'd had her fill of bile: "Days where I'm like, 'I need to take a break from the Internet. I am not going to look at comments. I'm not going to post anything. I need to leave for my own personal, self-care reasons.'" Phyllis, a White, libertarian activist in her 60s with the raspy, work-weary voice of a smoker, choked up as she spoke about the way the ugliness overwhelmed her: "You go through periods where you get pretty disgusted, pretty depressed and you just stop for a while. " She paused to gather herself, then continued: "That's why I sympathize with women because so many women, they just take this a few times and they say, "Well, that's enough. Why bother?"

Phyllis is right, breaks don't work for everyone. Several women spoke about leaving platforms they valued or retreating permanently into private accounts. Sophia left most social media, with the exception of a no-longer public Instagram account. Debbie password-protected her blog. Ruby sanitized her public Twitter account, which remains active, choosing only to express herself fully through a locked account with a just couple dozen approved followers. Coral quit blogging when it became too stressful to post. The list goes on.

Colu was very active on Instagram when she was younger, but repetitive, brutal comments about her appearance and body forced her off this once-cherished platform. In reflecting on how the identity-based attacks shaped her, Colu shared, "I realized I've become quiet and cautious online. So, my Instagram account, actually, had been closed for a really long time, because I felt like it was safer that way. I felt like you could protect yourself from online abuse, and stuff that way." She now maintains a tiny, private Instagram account, but the treatment spawned a generalized trepidation in other online spaces. These fears have been realized, across platforms, as she published her journalistic work.

Women are doing what they can to make the internet a safer space, but much of that work pulls them further away from freely participating in public discourse. In the most concerning cases, women decided to leave digital publics altogether. Several women I spoke with have watched other women leave. Lynette was deeply upset to see women around her leave:

> When you see some of the smartest women I know who no longer express an opinion in pubic, that's a painful, hurtful thing. I mean, I know some bad-ass women who, I'll see a conversation start to happen, for instance, I know someone right now who, her expertise is in constitution and intellectual property, which is not a common set of skills to have, and we're having this conversation right now about who owns what in the intellectual domain. She won't say anything publicly, and I don't blame her. Let's look at how many ways we lose when that's the case. The smartest person I know! I can't refer out to her on something that they know better than anybody else, because they've had enough.

"The ways we lose." What an important reminder of the value of diverse public debate. The women pushed out lose their voice, as do the rest of us who might benefit from their contributions. Hazel cried openly as she talked about the way trolls targeted the vocal women around her:

> They were going after [the most visible women], one by one. It started with going after [name redacted]. . . . They had run [another woman, name redacted] out of the industry with this playbook where it's like you go into a woman's past, you find something you can pull up against her to demonize her, and you attack, attack, attack, attack, attack until it's just not worth it to stay there. They did that to [her]. They did it to [another woman, name redacted]. They did it to [another, name redacted]. They did it to [another, name redacted]. They did it to [another, name redacted]. They did it to [still another, name redacted] and just one by one by one. They were coming at the most notable women in this field. If I ever end up leaving, it's not going

to be because they're going after me, it's going to be because my heart is broken from seeing them take out so many people I care about.

This phenomenon is one of the reasons Esther became involved in the fight against online harassment:

> When I started writing for [website, name redacted], there were a lot of people writing and there was a cultivated mob of men's rights activist commenters that migrated from platform to platform. Many people that were writing at the time, especially women, withdrew and refused to write anymore for [the site], because [the site was] not doing enough to moderate the content or to warn writers or to make a clear statement about . . . their ethos regarding some of these issues. . . . I was working with a publisher and a small committee of people to say, "Okay, what can we do about this problem? What is that boundary between free speech and commenting, between what writers say and what the discourse should be?" All of those things. A lot of women that I talked to in trying to work through that process basically said, "I'm not going to write for this [site] anymore, ever. Bye." Then a whole other group said, "I can't bear writing about certain topics because they're not safe. It's not safe for me to write about it and it makes life too difficult and unpleasant and my husband's fed up with me," or, "It makes me very upset," or, "I'm kind of really nervous every time I write something and I don't want to be that way." . . . It was very definitely linked to the hostility that they were experiencing. A lot of them, the hostility, as I mentioned, it didn't stay in that one place. Even if they stopped writing, the same group of people were now following them on Twitter or were reading what they were writing in other places and then commenting there. That was a problem. They were like, "I can't even escape this group of idiots anymore, because this is what they're doing."

The exodus Esther described aligns with some of the other stories I heard during the course of interviewing. Alongside those who were adamant that they would not be shamed and silenced out of public life, I met those who had decided to put their professional reputation, well-being, and safety ahead of their desire to speak out publicly. Selma, an Arabic academic researcher who identifies as mixed-race, told me that during the Arab Spring, she was very politically active on social media, serving as a conduit of information coming from people she knew in the region to those on the outside. She felt her role was critical amid rampant misinformation circulating in the news and on social media. Yet, the racist, Islamophobic, and misogynistic attacks were withering:

> What I really feel very strongly about is that no one's gonna curtail my right to talk about very sensitive topics and to use my, you know, intellect and professional opinion about these topics. I'm not gonna back down from talking about any of those topics. But I want to try to back off from having to experience crap being thrown at me because of who I am. So it's really, like, I don't know if I'm gonna ever succeed in this weird balancing act. But I just, I really feel like the price is too high. You can't expect . . . me to take all that crap. And maybe it will be in different phases. But I really felt like . . . even though I was in relatively controlled formats, the fact that these two websites just went on about me, it just, it really got to me. And getting just a couple of more racist, gendered comments directly affected me, you know, on Twitter or on my email, it's so little compared to what a lot of people have to deal with. But I just know that it's my vulnerability. It's something that I don't deal very well with. . . . So I don't want to make it worse for myself.

After the Arab Spring, Selma moved to less public venues with small audiences and no commenting. She hoped to feel safer, but was still attacked. Fearing the harassment might escalate, Selma no longer writes about Islam and the Middle East, and she has gravitated to private spaces:

> Everybody I know here who has gotten very involved in these types of topics, and has expressed their views in forums where the commentary is open, where anyone can comment anything, all of them have received rape threats. And I know that I don't want to put myself in that situation because I don't, I don't think I'm gonna handle it very well. . . . I am not going to put myself in situations where I will be, well, I know I will be the target. . . . I just think . . . I feel

like you have to have a little extra room in your life to deal with that kind of thing. I don't think I've had that for the last few years. So I feel like I have to do what I can to, like, participate in ways that don't cost me more than I have to give. . . . I think that if the general debate was less antagonistic and less personalized and definitely less related to my personal identity as a woman and as a woman of color, then I think I would participate much more actively in certain things. I wouldn't feel like I have to protect myself. . . . I've never been threatened for my life. And I think that's also related to the fact that I don't go into a lot of open forums where you can say whatever the hell you want. . . . I don't. . . . I don't want to be the person burdened with this.

Selma is an expert on these issues and cares about them. She wants to inform others and shape the conversation, but the identity-based attacks have worked. She told me she was no longer willing to be subjected the trolling:

My vulnerability is not my . . . It's not my views. It's who I am. So I don't have any problems expressing my views. It's that I don't want to . . . What's it called . . . I don't want to place myself in a situation where people get the chance to throw all their vile shit about me *at* me.

Parker also stepped away from the keyboard, and she mourned the opportunity she lost. At several points during our interview, she referenced what she might have done if not for the vicious, protracted campaign against her:

Terrorism is this strategy where you're trying to scare people into a behavior. I definitely felt scared. I can never hide my opinions because I'm a loud, brash person and I always will be. I definitely felt scared, and I guess still feel scared, to some extent, into compliance. Okay, so you don't want me to exist in public or else you're going to say these insane things and contact my employers? Okay, I will change my behavior online. I have a Facebook, my Facebook does not have my real name on it at all. It has definitely kept me from . . . I feel like there's an alternate universe version of me that would have . . . I wanted to be a journalist. I did work in journalism for about a year and a half. . . . This alternate version of me that has published books about feminism and has written articles.

Parker was clear-eyed and angry that she had been silenced. This anger weighted her words. She wanted it to sink in. She wanted me to understand, pausing for effect:

> For years, I didn't write it all. [Pause] For <u>years</u>. [Pause] . . . It's only now, recently, that I thought, "Hey, you know what? I have some job security now." . . . It's only now, really, that I thought, maybe I could write again.

Recall that she called it being terrorized into silence. Colu, too, has finished discussing political and social issues in public spaces. She still works as a journalist but told me that a rape threat made her rethink her publicness. When asked to elaborate, she said,

> So, I think there's a quote—and I'm not sure. I don't want to get it wrong. It might be by James Baldwin, but I'm not entirely sure. It's about the effects of a system, or whatever, is that when somebody is telling me what they would like to do to me . . . it comes to a point where you don't say something controversial, and no one has to tell you to shut up because you've told *yourself* to shut up. . . . So, I've told myself to shut up. . . . "It's not going to be worth it." And I think that's almost like a shadow over everything.

Aubrey used similar language when she told me the attackers "made a huge difference, I mean it's like . . . they've absolutely succeeded. I mean, people definitely succeeded in getting me to shut up about stuff, mostly because, after a point, you have to take care of yourself." Identity-based attacks matter. Women still talk about political and social issues in digital publics, but these abuse-induced departures show that digital hate has deleterious consequences.

As mentioned above, Rina stopped writing publicly about social inequality in gaming after being attacked. She wondered, though, if she went silent, if others who challenged toxic norms shut up, would things ever change?

I had sort of decreed, "I don't ever want to deal with this. This is gross and messy and this isn't what I do, and I don't want it to be what I do," but you kind of get just sucked into it, because then you have these moments where you're like, "but if I'm not saying it, is anyone saying it?" Somebody needs to say it. The reality is that people are saying it now, and I don't think that I'm needed for this. I don't feel like anyone needs me to be that voice. I suspect that if somebody *did* need me to be that voice, I would do it again, but . . . I'm not tenured yet, so I feel like there's a lot of risk in the choices of what I write about right now.

Rina's worry speaks directly to the concern at the center of this book. People are mean and abusive online. But the cruelty is not randomly distributed. Nor is the attrition.

SO WHAT?

Digital toxicity has prompted the some women in this book to stop writing about issues that animate them; some moderate their tone and their arguments to avoid abuse, some leave the platforms where their abuse coalesces, other take privacy breaks to recover from the fear and frustration, and hide behind identity-disguising avatars. Some withdraw into private digital spaces where they are surrounded by supportive peers. In the most concerning cases, women opt out of public discourse altogether. And, based on the uneven distribution of vitriol, it is likely that those who leave are disproportionately women who are of color, and/or queer, and/or Muslim, and so on. The most underrepresented voices and perspectives are likely to be the first pushed out. This matters. It violates the civil liberties of those targeted, creates barriers to representation and effective governance, and contributes to an information landscape that is already fraught with disinformation, misinformation, fake news, and propaganda.

CIVIL LIBERTIES

This abuse undermines the civil liberties of the women who are attacked and creates a chilling effect felt by other women who may pre-emptively decide it is too dangerous to be visible and vocal online. Research that has shown 41% of women between the ages of 15 and 29 self-censor to avoid online harassment, with some research finding even higher proportions (Lenhart et al. 2016; Olson and LaPoe 2017). In this regard, digital misogyny, like the threat of rape, even constrains the behavior of women who have not been attacked. Like the woman who avoids running alone at night for fear of attack, there are women who constrain their involvement in digital discourse because they fear backlash. This is especially true if the issues they wish to address are controversial, their views unpopular, or the conversation male-dominated. Cheryl, a magazine writer, speculated on what she called the "cost to women being drummed out of certain areas of discourse":

> If I'd been starting off on this profession, I don't know, maybe it would have, it depends on the person, I suppose. Maybe it would have made me go, "Wait a minute, first of all, journalism pays like shit. Second of all, I have to take all this abuse? Forget it." . . . There should be freedom of opportunity for women and men to do anything they want to do, and to women who want to do hard-hitting journalism or science writing or whatever. It bums me out that some women would be scared off of that, that a teenage girl who was the editor for a high school paper would hear about some of this stuff and go, "Forget it, I'm not . . ." That's too bad, because good journalists—we need all kinds of perceptive people, of different genders, backgrounds, sexual orientations and if only men wrote about science—not to get too misty-eyed about "women's perspectives are helpful," blah, blah, blah, but I do think that there are different ways of thinking and that your gender does sometimes affect those ways of thinking and that we need smart people of all kinds writing about issues of all kinds. I think that there is a cost to women being drummed out of certain areas of discourse.

Cheryl's speculation is supported by the accounts in this book. Women are scared. Headline-making cases of abuse such as the Gamer Gate attacks on Anita Sarkeesian, Zoe Quinn, and Brianna Wu; haranguing of feminist writer Caroline Criado Perez; and threats against Professor Christine Blassey-Ford after her testimony in front of the US Senate Judiciary Committee have made wide swaths of women aware that digital violence is a clear, constant, and credible threat. The awareness that attacks can escalate, that there is always the potential for the hostility to become all-consuming, shapes the choices women make online.

As a young Black woman, Annelise is familiar with a repertoire of imper-sonal, yet intensely intimate abuse. Among other things, she is called a Black bitch, the c-word, and the n-word. She receives pornographic gifs and is told to "go back to Africa." She is referred to as delusional and hysterical, sent dick pics, and jeered as fat and ugly. At times, she told me, it feels like the 1800s. Few seem to take seriously the vitriol with which she contends; they write it off as "people being mean." But Annelise sees something much bigger at play and wants the torment recognized as consequential:

> It's a public space issue. It's a public space issue and a public safety issue, and it's also a free speech and free expression issue. . . . [Stopping online harassment is] about ending the silencing, systematically, of women, people of color, and other underrepresented groups. . . . Even though harassment or violence is happening in online space, it doesn't mean it's not violence. When President Obama, at South by Southwest, referred to online harassment as violence against women and violence in public space, that was a win for all of us, because we were like okay! We have done our job in shifting this framing to this degree. There's so much work to still do, but to the degree that the President of the United States is now acknowledging it's a pub-lic safety issue. And I think the connection that needs to be made for a lot of people is the fact that the most egregious forms of online harassment are impacting women and people of color. So, the doxx-ing, the violent attacks and threats, et cetera, which is something a lot of people don't know. They think that you're just upset about mean speech.

It is more than sticks and stones for Annelise, as it is for Selma, who is stunned that such behaviors are happening in societies that fancy themselves egalitar-ian, "In the big picture . . . what I think is a huge problem, [female] politicians, everybody who has a public voice are receiving these kinds of violent threats. Women who speak their mind are receiving rape threats. Also, in societies where you would expect that this could not even happen!" For all of the con-cern about freedom of speech and expression, few seem attentive to the ways that digital hate tramples women's ability to speak freely.

The threat of digital harassment constrains women's voice and visibility and hence their ability to participate in political and cultural life. This may have long-term effects for underrepresented groups. Debbie worries that the toxicity undermines the ability of those from underrepresented groups to fight for justice by driving them out of public debate:

> In general, people don't understand that it's a gendered phenomenon. I don't think they believe it. I also think that a lot of people think of it as a First Amendment issue. It ends up foreclosing any kind of consideration of the negative effects it might be having on certain targeted groups. . . . The few voices who are out there, the few voices that are prominent in communities of color, for example, the trans community, are probably getting it worse than anyone can imagine. I know for a fact it has a silencing effect, too. I know women who won't engage. They're just not on social media because of it. Of course, I see [the social media] as a tool, and it's really important. It's become increasingly important for activism. I worry, too, that [digital abuse] might be silencing—It might be [hurting] activism, because women don't want to face the sexism online.

Debbie wants people to understand that the patterned nature of the venom is linked to differential attrition. And Esther is fed up with the knee-jerk response to online harassment, at least in the United States, which tends to collapse conversations by referencing freedom of speech. "What about women's speech?" she asked with disdain.

> We're not capturing the loss of speech that *we're* talking about. We know that girls and women have these security concerns. We know that they're not engaging in political debate. We know that they experience harassment in different ways and that it's more emotionally taxing. How do we capture that?

Debbie and Esther asked poignant questions about how marginalization shapes women's involvement and why so few seem to truly care. They wondered how it will shape the way social and political issues are understood and addressed going forward.

WHO LEADS AND HOW?

One likely consequence is that some women will be scared out of the pool of future leaders. Emma Gonzalez, whose online abuse opened this book, is not the only activist who has been harangued by digital misogyny. Conservative singer and activist Joy Villa was targeted with identity-based attacks after wearing political dresses supporting the US/Mexico border wall and opposing Planned Parenthood on the red carpet (Moniuszko 2019), and teen climate activist Greta Thunberg is also a frequent target of trolls, who often target her physical appearance and mock her for having Asperger's Syndrome. Activists today need social media; Visibility on Twitter, for example, helps put activism in the news, ultimately attracting the attention of decision makers (Freelon, McIlwain, and Clark 2018).

In August 2018, with an unprecedented number of women running for public office in the United States, the *New York Times* released a video featuring current and former female political candidates talking about their experiences with harassment and sexism, much via social media, during their campaigns (Kerr, Tiefenthaler, and Fineman 2018). In the video, the women describe gendered and racialized abuse. Among the women featured is Iowa Democrat Kim Weaver, who pulled out of her 2016 congressional race amid a torrent of sexist and anti-Semitic abuse (Astor 2018). And the evidence is not just anecdotal: rigorous research has shown that the abuse is systematic and continues even after its targets take office. Being politically vocal online brings abuse to women in positions of power, especially when they are women of color (Sobieraj and Merchant forthcoming; Rheault, Rayment, and Musulan 2019). In other words, even privileged women in positions of authority find their credibility, worth, and words undermined by gender-based abuse and threats too often dismissed as normal discourse. If they can't stand the heat, many seem to say, these women should just get out of the kitchen—or Congress.

This could become—perhaps it already is—another barrier to women's representation in politics (Southern and Harmer 2019). Among recent headline-making attacks, we can cite US Representatives Ilhan Omar (D-MN) and Alexandria Ocasio-Cortez (D-NY), both of whom have endured venomous identity-based abuse online. And in late 2019, 18 female members of Britain's Parliament decided not to run for re-election, citing rape threats, abuse, and "sexually-charged rhetoric" on and offline as the reason for their departure. MP Heidi Allen wrote to her constituents, "Nobody in any job should have to put up with threats, aggressive emails, being shouted at in the street, sworn at on social media, nor have to install panic alarms at home" (Scott 2019; Specia 2019). Even those with little concern for gender or racial equality know that shrinking the talent pool (perhaps the purpose behind much of the abuse) is a concerning development. For those from historically marginalized groups who are hungry to be truly *represented* by their representatives, this is particularly devastating.

MISINFORMATION, DISINFORMATION, LIMITED INFORMATION, AND DEMOCRACY

Barriers to access and legitimacy in digital publics recall features of exclusionary publics that long predate digital technologies. History has already shown us the epistemological costs of patterned exclusion. Histories of White, landowning, male deliberation have already shown how severely the products of social and political dialogue are distorted when the things we come to believe as truths or facts or reality are by definition incomplete, because members of specific groups of society have been systematically pushed out of public conversations (Sobieraj 2019). Our ability to innovate, understand social problems, work together, and build effective policies hinges on a steady supply of rich and reliable information from diverse sources.

It stands to reason, for example, that effective approaches to health care need to be informed by the experiences of those who lack, use, and provide that care. Consider Serena Williams's public discussion of her near-fatal pulmonary embolism. The athlete has a history of these artery blockages in her lungs, so she knew what was happening when the symptoms started just after she gave birth. Gasping for air, Williams informed a nurse that she needed an intravenous blood thinner and a CT (computerized tomography) scan right away. Instead of calling for help, the nurse dismissed her concerns as "confusion" related to pain medication and ordered an unnecessary ultrasound of her legs. Williams insisted to the medical team that it was her lungs and she needed help, but it was not until the ultrasound came up short that Williams was given a CT scan that identified several small clots in her lungs (Haskell 2018). Later, Williams amplified her story across platforms, sitting for interviews with legacy media, writing an opinion piece for CNN.com, and posting to Facebook and Twitter in order to call attention to the minimization of Black women's pain and racial bias in maternity treatment, both of which are linked to preventable deaths (Lockhart 2018). Williams's outspoken response encouraged other women to come forward with their stories, propelled a ProPublica and NPR report on Black women's childbirth-related deaths into the headlines, brought attention to the role of practitioners' implicit bias in the poor maternal outcomes of Black women, and prompted Senator

Kamala Harris (D-CA) to introduce the Maternal Care Access and Reducing Emergencies (CARE) Act ("Sen. Harris Introduces Bill Aimed at Reducing Racial Disparities in Maternal Mortality" 2018; Reinstein 2018; Martin and Montagne 2017). Williams proved pivotal in opening the door for stories from journalists, researchers, and other Black women that coalesced to form a striking snapshot of a widespread problem.

Black women's disproportionate number of childbirth-related deaths has long been known, but little had been done to explore or address the complex factors contributing to their fatalities. The Centers for Disease Control and Prevention, for example, has a Pregnancy Mortality Surveillance System that compiles related data. The CDC's discussion of the monitoring system and the data it has generated includes a visual depicting dramatic racial and ethnic disparities in mortality, but the only reference to the inequality reads, "Variability in the risk of death by race/ethnicity indicates that more can be done to understand and reduce pregnancy-related deaths." The remainder of the CDC discussion treats the causes of and risk factors for pregnancy-related deaths as race-neutral ("Pregnancy Mortality Surveillance System" 2020). Further, the CDC discussion focuses on lifestyle choices and pre-existing conditions, without raising questions related to equitable care. This is but one example of the larger point: the knowledge on which we base our policies is able to be more comprehensive, meaningful, and accurate when our public conversations are inclusive.

The women in this research must be included. They are offering important perspectives, discussing issues in new ways, and, especially in the case of academics and journalists, often asking questions and writing about topics that have long been overlooked. They are, as their critics resent, destabilizers. This is not to say that they are always right or that their approaches are superior to those with longer histories in the public eye, but we, as a public, are better for the opportunity to consider a wide range of information and arguments. Patterned gaps in the perspectives to which we have access, such as those likely to emerge in response to the resistance described in this book, reduce the breadth and depth of the information we have available when we make personal choices and political decisions, and when those in positions of influence build and re-build public policies.

Identity-based attacks deal a second blow to information quality by weaponizing disinformation and misinformation as part and parcel of their abuse. Many of the women in this study were distraught to find outlandish lies posted about them. Some discovered websites created solely to defame them. When disinformation is circulated about activists, journalists, candidates, and public servants, it damages the targets' reputations and our collective information landscape.

Representative Omar is one of just two Muslim women in the US Congress. She has been pummeled by Islamophobic, racist, xenophobic, ageist, and sexist attacks online since entering the political arena. Disinformation has played a central role. US President Donald Trump has fanned the flames by, for instance, tweeting in July 2019, that " 'Progressive' Democrat Congresswomen" "go back and help fix the totally broken and crime infested places from which they came. Then come back and show us how it is done." In response, Omar tweeted a segment of Maya Angelou's (1978) defiant poem, "Still I Rise": "You may shoot me with your words, You may cut me with your eyes, You may kill me with your hatefulness, But still, like air, I'll rise."

Omar used Angelou's message to assert her resilience, but some set out to put her public display of strength to the test. Among the replies to Omar's tweet were accusations that she had married her brother, a three-year-old unfounded conspiracy. Others insisted that Omar was a terrorist, an argument that gained traction online after being posed by conservative agitator Glenn Beck. Inspired by Beck, *Front Page* ran one story titled, "CONGRESSWOMAN ILHAN OMAR: TERRORIST," which gained nearly 60,000 shares on Facebook alone. Attackers repeated claims, insults, and innuendoes, proliferating them across platforms. Others lobbed recirculated falsehoods, like the debunked rumor that Omar would not pledge allegiance to America during her inauguration. And at moments the digital attacks introduced new "facts" into the conversation; among the replies to her Maya Angelou tweet were those who insisted that she tortures, guts, and eats children; has been personally involved in the massacre of Somalis; and is a "fake citizen" sent to start a war to destroy the United States (Sobieraj 2019). This kind of disinformation cuts twice: it both fuels the rage directed at its target and makes the subsequent rumors seem more plausible. The more a piece of misinformation is repeated, the more likely we are to believe that it is true (Claypool et al. 2004; Fazio, Rand, and Pennycook 2019; Foster et al. 2012; Pennycook, Cannon, and Rand 2018).

As outrageous as these comments seem, they have consequences. Omar has had to address these claims ad nauseum. During the 2018 election season, for instance, she told the *Star Tribune*, "It's really strange, right, to prove a negative." In reference to the incest allegations, she said, "If someone was asking me, do I have a brother by that name, I don't. If someone was asking . . . are there court documents that are false . . . there is no truth to that." And yet, like Birther conspiracy theories leveled against Barack Obama, these questions persist.

In December 2019, *The Guardian* reported that an Israeli-based group had been using Facebook to spread disinformation about Omar to more than a million followers around the world (Smith et al. 2019). Reputation management takes time and energy, and the rumors distract constituents, colleagues, and journalists from focusing on issues that Omar feels are more salient. They surely distract *her* from doing important work as a political leader. And the fear-mongering may cost her re-election. But this is hardly a *personal problem*. Disinformation and misinformation are antithetical to a healthy information environment, and democratic elections are only meaningful if the citizenry has adequate information to make informed decisions on their own behalf when they enter the voting booth.

Unacceptable Outcomes

Robust democracies are built on political discourse in which people—including those without power—respectfully discuss even the most sensitive topics (e.g., immigration, abortion, guns, race) and share their ideas, experience, and opinions without fear. The hostile climate with which these women contend undermines this possibility at the precise moment in history when realizing this vision would otherwise be most viable. The same internet and communications technologies that vastly improved both access and opportunities for inclusive participation have been weaponized against those who need them most. Identity-based attacks ultimately wreak havoc in women's lives, create a chilling effect even for women who have not been attacked, and abrade democratic vitality. They do so by wearing away the civil liberties that serve as the foundation of democracy, turning activism and public service into unappealing, high-risk endeavors, diminishing the validity of the knowledge that informs policy, and promoting an ill-informed electorate.

Conclusions

Resilience Isn't Enough

Between July and September of 2019, Facebook "took action" on 7 million pieces of content identified as hate speech and over 3 million pieces linked to bullying and harassment ("Facebook Transparency Report: Community Standards Enforcement" 2019). In talking about the challenge of keeping people safe online, Del Harvey, director of Trust and Safety at Twitter, has said, "Given the scale that Twitter is at, a one-in-a-million chance happens five hundred times a day. It's the same for other companies dealing at this sort of scale. For us, edge cases, those rare situations that are unlikely to occur, are more like norms" (Harvey 2014). These *are* norms. And they are norms that threaten the security of female users (particularly those from underrepresented groups), the vitality of our public spheres, and ultimately the health of democracy. Digital abuse has been noted in arenas ranging from gaming (Gray 2012; 2014; Fox and Tang 2017) to academia (Ferber 2018; Veletsianos et al. 2018), journalism (Chen et al. 2018; Adams 2018; Gardiner 2018), and politics (Kerr, Tiefenthaler, and Fineman 2018; Rheault, Rayment, and Musulan 2019; Sobieraj and Merchant forthcoming). Whether you are listening to social media firms, academic researchers, or the women in this study, it is clear that digital abuse against women is widespread and deeply disruptive.

For too long, digital attacks have been mistaken for what C. Wright Mills (1959) called *personal troubles*. A personal trouble is a problem linked to an individual's character, choices, and immediate surroundings. As such, they are best resolved by the individual using the resources at their disposal. Public issues also create problems that affect individuals, but in contrast to personal

Credible Threat. Sarah Sobieraj, Oxford University Press (2020). © Oxford University Press.
DOI: 10.1093/oso/9780190089283.001.0001.

troubles, these problems are rooted in social structures and institutional arrangements. As a result, public issues can only be resolved by changing the institutions and structures that generate them. Individual efforts may ameliorate the problem or shift the burden to someone else, but the cause remains, and so the public issues persist.

Women on the receiving end of digital toxicity undertake Herculean efforts to minimize the costs of participating in public conversations of political and social importance. These survival tactics are essential in a context that fails to take their abuse seriously, but they are rarely effective, because digital abuse can only be addressed meaningfully through systemic solutions.

Legal Holes

In the case of the United States, where most of my respondents are based, the legal system fails to deter most abusive behavior. As addressed in Chapter 2, victims may pursue a variety of criminal and civil actions. Unfortunately, these perpetrator-centered laws are ill-suited to digital harassment in which harassers can be hard to identify and where the abuse often comes in the form of a million paper cuts—few of which individually meet the thresholds set by criminal and tort law. And even in cases where the thresholds are met, jurisdictional issues often complicate prosecution.

For their part, the Federal Bureau of Investigation (FBI) has begun to address "cyber crime," but the identity-based attacks described by my participants fall beyond its scope of concern. The FBI's "Cyber Crime" website lists the bureau's priorities: computer and network intrusions, ransomware, identity theft, and child predators ("Cyber Crime" n.d.). And its Internet Crime Complaint Center (IC3) accepts complaints related to Internet crime, but defines these crimes narrowly:

> Internet crime includes any illegal activity involving one or more components of the Internet, such as websites, chat rooms, and/or email. Internet crime involves the use of the Internet to communicate false or fraudulent representations to consumers. These crimes may include, but are not limited to, advance-fee schemes, non-delivery of goods or services, computer hacking, or employment/business opportunity schemes. ("Internet Crime Complaint Center (IC3)" n.d.)

If someone tries to trick you out of your money, you can file a complaint, but if and angry mob of strangers are trying to terrify you into hiding, you'll need to go elsewhere.

If there is a bright spot in this grim legal context, it is around the distribution of nonconsensual pornography (NCP), commonly, if sometimes erroneously, referred to as "revenge pornography." At the time of this writing, 46 US states have enacted laws prohibiting the distribution of nude images without the depicted person's consent. Federal laws are poised to follow. Senator Kamala Harris (D-CA) has, for instance, reintroduced the SHIELD (Stopping Harmful Image Exploitation and Limiting Distribution) Act, which would criminalize the act of knowingly sharing sexually explicit or nude images without consent. These emerging laws are important and represent an effort to build the kinds of structures necessary to support victims. NCP was weaponized against three of the women in this research; unfortunately, in none of those cases is there a known perpetrator to charge. And although similar in many ways to NCP, the distribution of falsified pornographic images, such as those used to humiliate several of my respondents, falls beyond the reach of such laws. In other words, the NCP laws are important tools in cases of intimate, interpersonal harassment, but they have largely symbolic value for cases in which the abuse is meted out by strangers en masse.

Civil rights laws, designed to punish abuse motivated by race, national origin, religion, and (in some states) gender and sexual orientation, have not yet been embraced as a form of redress, according the legal scholar Danielle Citron. She suggests that, to the extent that online harassment threatens to drive people from protected groups offline, civil rights law has some potential heft, yet "law cannot communicate norms, deter unlawful activity, or remedy injuries if defendants cannot be found. Perpetrators can be hard to identify if they use anonymizing technologies or post on sites that do not collect IP addresses. Because the law's efficacy depends on having defendants to penalize, legal reform should include, but not focus exclusively on, harassers" (2014, 143). The most effective path toward eliminating digital abuse, she emphasizes, is unlikely to be one that hinges on catching individual attackers.

Platform Accountability

Identity-based attacks are transmitted via email, mobile messaging, chat rooms, discussion boards, comment sections, and websites built explicitly to attack. But most of the abuse comes via major social media platforms such as Facebook, YouTube, and Twitter. If intervening attacker by attacker is not viable, these platforms—the vehicles by which the abuse is delivered—are the most appropriate point of intervention.

In the United States, where these platforms are based, they are legally considered *online intermediaries* rather than *publishers*, because they are primarily conduits for content created, shared, and/or curated by others rather than spaces designed to produce and showcase their own content. This is not to say that platforms are neutral or impartial. On the contrary, platforms organize, filter, moderate, and highlight content. Platforms also have design features, or affordances, that shape the way users interact with the content they encounter—and with one another. All this is done in the name of optimizing the user experience—by displaying the content that users are most interested in seeing—but these features are also intended to increase time on site, engagements, click-throughs, and other behaviors that appeal to advertisers and raise revenue for the platforms (Gillespie 2018a; 2018b; Klonick 2018; Vaidhyanathan 2018).

As intermediaries, social media platforms enjoy broad immunity from liability for the content shared by their users. This immunity is granted by Section 230 of the Communications Decency Act of 1996. Section 230 releases intermediaries from the need to monitor user content, while also providing legal room so that they *may* monitor user content as they see fit (Gillespie 2018a; Klonick 2018). Twitter and Facebook, like most social media companies, are privately owned. They can remove content they find in violation of their community standards or policies, but they are not *required* to moderate the content they host. Nor can they, under US law, be held liable for hosting or pushing terrorist propaganda, hate speech, disinformation, or other objectionable content into their users' feeds.

These feeds increase in importance as major social media platforms swell in popularity. Facebook dominates the social media landscape, with nearly 2.4 billion users worldwide. But YouTube is nearing 2 billion users of its own and several other platforms have between 500 million and 1 billion users, including Instagram and Tumblr (Ortiz-Espina 2019). Content moderation expert, Tarleton Gillespie argues, "When an intermediary grows this large, this entwined with the institutions of public discourse, this crucial, it has an *implicit contract* with the public. . . . The primary and secondary effects these platforms have on essential aspects of public life, as they become apparent, now lie at their doorstep" (2018b, 208). Thus far, platforms such as Twitter,

Facebook, and YouTube have been unable or unwilling to manage the emergent threats posed by harassment such as civil rights abuses, reductions in information diversity, or the circulation of disinformation. It is clear that industry self-regulation of harmful content—the de facto norm in the United States, as a result of Section 230 of the Communications Decency Act of 1996—is no longer in the public interest.

Europe and Australia have been more open to state intervention in internet content, particularly around hate speech. In 2019, after Brenton Harrison Tarrant livestreamed his deadly attack on two mosques in Christchurch, New Zealand, several governments intervened. The footage, shared millions of times, led several leaders to lash out, accusing social media platforms of insufficient efforts to stop circulating hate. France passed a landmark law requiring that social media companies remove "obviously hateful" content within 24 hours or face stiff fines (*The Guardian* 2019). In Germany, platforms already faced penalties of up to 50 million euros for failing to promptly remove hate speech, and lawmakers are poised to vote on rules requiring social media platforms to "proactively report illegal content such as death threats or incitement of hatred on their platforms to law enforcement" (Scott and Delcker 2019). And at the time of this writing, Australia is in the public comment period of a new Online Safety Act aimed to, among other purposes, "facilitate the removal of serious online abuse and harassment and introduce a new end user take-down and civil penalty regime" and establish "consistent take-down requirements for image-based abuse, cyber abuse, cyberbullying and seriously harmful online content, requiring online service providers to remove such material within 24 hours" (Department of Infrastructure 2019).

There are good reasons to be wary of imposing content-related regulations on social media platforms. Some regimes relish the opportunity to determine what kind of speech counts as hateful or harmful and use pro-social sounding laws as a guise to quash opposition. As I write, for example, the Nigerian senate is considering a proposed National Commission for the Prohibition of Hate Speech bill, with penalties including imprisonment or death, as well as the Protection from Internet Falsehood and Manipulation and Other Related Offences bill, which Amnesty International suggests could limit social media or internet access ("Nigeria Is Considering Incredibly Harsh Punishments for Social Media Users Who Criticize the Government" 2019). In the United States, where hateful speech is protected by the First Amendment to the Constitution, such blatant and state-centered censorship strikes a particularly discordant note. Here, where both individual speech and business rights are paramount, government intervention into privately owned public spheres feels understandably fraught with political risk.

First Amendment arguments are especially challenging. Censorship surely limits free speech. But so does digital hate. Women who come under attack see their civil liberties curtailed, even when the censorship and exclusion from public dialog is self-imposed. If such withdrawal is a behavior necessary to limit threats in the face of reluctance to limit the speech of abusers, this reluctance prioritizes the speech rights of attackers over those who are targeted. Though the argument can be—and often is—twisted, we must be clear: reining in patterned toxicity offers meaningful benefits with minimal loss. Despite the obfuscating arguments presented by platforms, most identity-based attacks fall under the umbrella of "low-value" speech, which can be regulated—even in the United States—because its power to cause harm outweighs its value. True threats, speech that incites criminal conduct, defamation, obscenity, and the imminent and likely incitement of violence, are not given the same First Amendment protections as other forms of speech (Citron 2014). Further, civil rights abuses are *not* protected by the First Amendment. Citron explains, "When law punishes online attackers due to their singling out victims for online abuse due to their gender, race, sexual orientation, or other protected characteristic and the special severity of the harm produced, and not due to the particular opinions that the attackers or victims express, its application does not transgress the First Amendment" (2014, 221). Remember, the abuse shouts: "This is a woman." "You are a woman." "She is a woman." That this abuse is about these victims as women—as queer women, Black women, Muslim women (and in some cases as queer Black Muslim women)—is self-evident. These attacks are about bringing these devalued identities to the fore in the interest of power. They are *fundamentally* about limiting the voice and impact of specific groups of people in the public sphere. This is not the kind of speech the First Amendment sought to preserve.

The Governors

If ever there were a time to address platform accountability, this is it. We are in the midst of what has been dubbed a "techlash." Public concern about the role of major technology companies in society has reached a boiling point. Facebook is under what seems like constant fire. In 2019, the tech giant paid a record-breaking $5 billion civil settlement to the Federal Trade Commission

(FTC) over alleged[1] data and privacy issues (Kelly 2019). The industry leader paid another $100 million to the Securities and Exchange Commission for misleading investors about the privacy breach. YouTube settled its own 2019 FTC suit for $170 million for violating children's privacy, while Amazon and Google joined Facebook in the FTC crosshairs for potential anti-trust violations (Isaac and Kang 2019). Perhaps most interestingly, the techlash has become politically popular with a range of legislators who otherwise agree on little. Among the platform critics are senators Elizabeth Warren (D-MA), Ted Cruz (R-TX), Bernie Sanders (I-VT), Amy Klobuchar (D-MN), and Josh Hawley (R-MO). In perhaps the gravest news for Silicon Valley yet, US Attorney General William Barr indicated at the end of 2019 that the Justice Department would be revisiting the blanket immunity provided by Section 230 (Romm 2019).

These country-level interventions are part and parcel of an emergent global call for platform governance linking together deeply felt concerns about a comprehensive set of harms. This includes harassment and abuse, but also phenomena including issues as diverse as governance of artificial intelligence, information quality, anti-trust concerns, data rights, and privacy issues (Owen 2019). It seems that platforms will face increased oversight, but what is less clear is who the overseers will be. In the sphere of hate speech, efforts have been initiated by governments, civil society organizations, and even the platforms themselves.

The most visible of the government-led initiatives is the European Union's Code of Conduct on Illegal Hate Speech Online, which was created in 2016. This voluntary transnational code emerged from a collaborative forum featuring EU governments and several major tech companies (including Facebook, YouTube, Instagram, Google+, Twitter, and Microsoft). The code defines hate speech as "all conduct publicly inciting to violence or hatred directed against a group of persons or a member of such a group defined by reference to race, colour, religion, descent or national or ethnic origin" (2016, 1) and argues for the enforcement of existing EU regulations. Under the agreement, the platforms affirmed that they would remove illegal hate speech violating their Terms of Service within 24 hours of reporting. Relatedly, Citron (2018) reports that the platforms have adjusted their global Terms of Service to align with the interests of the EU. The tech companies signed this voluntary agreement pre-emptively, as a way to ward off more invasive regulations.

Perhaps it will be the third sector that ends up regulating digital hate. The Global Network Initiative (GNI) emerged in 2008 and responded to what was then seen as the pre-eminent threat to free speech globally: governments. According to its website, "GNI helps companies respect freedom of expression and privacy rights when faced with government pressure to hand over user data, remove content, or restrict communications." The GNI used international human rights law to create a set of principles. Each signatory affirms and agrees to implement the GNI's principles, which include an accountability plan outlining a system of compliance and oversight (Gorwa 2019).

A decade on, when the tech companies are themselves increasingly viewed as needing regulation, civil society groups have taken up a somewhat different framing. ARTICLE 19, a prominent free speech organization, has proposed creating Social Media Councils (SMCs) focused on content moderation. These councils (which could be regional, national, or transnational) would be composed of stakeholders including representatives from civic groups, minority and vulnerable communities, social media companies, journalists, academia, public media, and advertisers. An independent forum, the SMCs could make recommendations related to content moderation (both pre-emptively and as an appellate body) in an inclusive, transparent, and judicious manner with an eye toward protecting freedom of expression (Doquir 2019; Tworek 2019). This is a delicate balance, as ARTICLE 19's website makes clear:

> Hate and discrimination present increasing challenges to ensuring that all people are able to enjoy their right to freedom of expression, and other human rights, equally. Removing discriminatory barriers so that all people can speak out and be heard, and ensuring that no one is censored on the basis of who they are, is central to securing the right to freedom of expression. "Hate speech," as a form of discriminatory expression, is a serious human rights concern. It is a tool often used to silence and intimidate minorities, and to scapegoat whole groups in society while stifling dissent.... Broadly framed "hate speech" laws are also frequently misapplied to target minority and dissenting expression. ARTICLE 19 advocates for States to engage in a range of law and policy measures to counter "hate speech" with more speech, seeking to maximise inclusivity, diversity and pluralism in public discourse. That means clearly defining the circumstances in which certain types of "hate speech" can or must be limited, and ensuring those measures are only used exceptionally, and as a last resort. ("Equality and Hate Speech" n.d.)

Curtailing free speech, even hate speech, it emphasizes, must be but a "last resort." The SMC model was endorsed by United Nations Special Rapporteur David Kaye and will likely be in a pilot stage around the time this book goes to press. As with the GNI, it relies on voluntary platform compliance (Doquir 2019).

This brings us back to the failure of platform self-regulation to solve issues related to harassment and hate speech. Facebook CEO Mark Zuckerberg responded to the techlash in late 2019, announcing the establishment of an independent (or at least quasi-independent) external Oversight Board to advise the platform on content policy and adjudicate content removal appeals. The board will be made up of independent experts, serving three-year terms, and it will be financially independent. Its decisions related to user content will be binding. The board can also recommend policy changes. Facebook is not required to comply, but should the company decline, it must provide a public explanation for that decision (Klonick 2018). No other platform has undertaken such a considerable reimagining of the content moderation process.[2] The success, failure, and overall reception of the Oversight Board is likely to be pivotal in shaping how other industry leaders address moderation going forward.

In the meantime, other platforms are constantly tweaking and expanding their policies to craft maximum flexibility while attempting to placate critics. Twitter's hateful conduct policy now prohibits, for example, language that dehumanizes others on the basis of religion, while YouTube has updated its harassment policy to include veiled threats and personal attacks against users and comment creators alike. (At last, recognition that threats need not be credible to be deeply upsetting.) Both changes came only after months of fits and starts in which changes to hate speech policies were rolled out, retracted, changed, and relaunched. These are bold moves, but whether they will be adequately enforced such that they are anything more than symbolic measures remains to be seen. Two months after the YouTube crackdown that banned videos containing white supremacist content as well as videos denying well-documented atrocities including the Holocaust and the Sandy Hook shooting, the Anti-Defamation League Center on Extremism identified 29 anti-Semitic and White Supremacist channels still striving and thriving on the platform ("Despite YouTube Policy Update, Anti-Semitic, White Supremacist Channels Remain" 2019).

It's Not Illegal to Be an Asshole

It is encouraging that concerns about digital toxicity have entered the zeitgeist (even Melania Trump's *Be Best* campaign addressed online safety). An array of efforts that hope to divine innovative and meaningful approaches to the problem are under way. But, at the end of the day, will any of this actually work for the women in this research?

Yes and no. More inclusive platform policies, such as Twitter's rejection of dehumanization on the basis of religion and YouTube's attention to veiled threats, are important. Those policies, alongside new laws criminalizing the distribution of NCP, send a powerful message. They mark this mistreatment as unacceptable, provide victims with a language to help outsiders understand their plight, and offer a path toward recourse. Were social media platforms to lose the broad immunity afforded by Section 230, women who have been harmed as a result of negligence in policy enforcement may be able to bring civil suits against them. Further, if corporate behavior in other contexts is any indication, the fear of such litigation might motivate platforms to invest in higher quality content moderation. At the same time, it could lead companies to abandon moderation completely, leaving a climate so toxic that users and advertisers flee for friendlier landscapes.

However, promising these developments, identity-based attacks would still be challenging to curb. For example, it's neither illegal nor against policy to be an asshole. And, of course, it shouldn't be. But that means that a significant portion of the attacks would still be permitted. Hurtful stereotypes (e.g., invoking gender race, ethnicity, class, etc.), identity-based epithets (in many contexts), detailed commentary on women's physical appearance, and conjecture about their sexual behaviors and preferences are still going to greet women when they enter digital publics. And unless something changes, women are still going to need to see, flag, and report the shocking content that meets the threshold for removal. In other words, the changes underfoot at this juncture will do nothing to make the climate less hostile or to free them from hand-wringing and self-surveillance in advance of publishing or the subsequent ameliorative work. While in most cases platforms are a better point of entry than law enforcement, at the end of the day, the abuse is a deeply rooted product of misogyny, white supremacy, xenophobia, and other inequalities that platforms may unintentionally support, but they did not invent.

Pre-emptive moderation, whether via artificial intelligence or human judgment, appears to be the only way to create distance between the vitriol and the target. Social Media Councils and Oversight Boards are primarily adjudicative, not preventive. If, however, through their role as policy advisors, these bodies steer platforms toward pre-moderation, there may be hope. The problem of scale is well-documented—and many invoke it to argue that pre-emptive review is impossible—but hybrid models are conceivable. For example, some systems already allow for users to earn their way out of pre-moderation by establishing a track record of posting content in keeping with community standards. Other platforms might pre-moderate at random, reducing the workload dramatically. Effectively, pre-moderating disincentivizes posting content that violates community standards because, if no one will see it, why bother? With a hybrid system, flagging and reporting remain in place as back-ups, not first-line defenses. And none of this is to minimize the outsized effort and investment that even a hybrid system would require, nor the daunting implications for those who would ultimately do the work of pre-moderation. As Information Studies scholar Sarah Roberts (2019) shows, the labor of moderation is harrowing yet tedious, often requiring a relentless pace and exposure to horrific content at low wages.

What about Fatima, Debbie, and Lynette?

As we work toward creating healthier speaking environments, we must simultaneously work to build ameliorative infrastructure to support the victims of identity-based attacks. Too many women in this research reached out for help only to find friends, family, employers, and law enforcement at a loss. If we center victims in our thinking, it becomes easy to envision concrete steps we might take to lessen the impact of this abuse.

Supporting those who are attacked requires first and foremost that we name and acknowledge the problem. Recognizing acquaintance rape and domestic violence as social problems proved pivotal in helping women understand and find support for experiences previously discounted as insignificant or deemed the product of victims' risky choices. Digital abuse and harassment must also be added to our cultural lexicon.

Beyond a name, the abuse needs to be better understood. To really "see" digital abuse means recognizing several characteristics that are often lost.

First, that digital attacks are disruptive to victims' lives, in that they are often onerous, distressing, embarrassing, and dangerous. Second, it requires understanding that it is the cumulative effect of digital attacks that exact a toll. As a result, the behaviors of individual attackers and the content of isolated messages, posts, or emails may appear insignificant to outsiders, but they still play a role in the victim's experience. Third, while online toxicity can be directed at anyone, it must become clear that it is most often directed at women, especially those from underrepresented groups, who are attacked in ways that center their identities (e.g., gender, racial, ethnic, religious, sexual). Finally, we need public recognition that this harassment not only complicates their ability to participate fully and express themselves freely online, but it also discourages other women from entering the conversation. As such, digital abuse and harassment impinge on victims' civil rights and on the quality of our public discourse writ large.

Creating a shared language around what it means to be targeted online will help advocates press for improved institutional responses that center victims. For example, policymakers and activists would be well served to press law enforcement to develop new protocols for handling complaints about digital abuse. Even in contexts such as the United States, where much of the abuse will not be legally actionable, responding officers can play an important role in supporting victims. Helping officers become well versed on attackers' tactics and the primary venues for online hostility is an important first step. Too many women in this sample described needing to explain to officers how Twitter works or what a direct message is in the middle of a crisis. Implementing protocols that emphasize sensitivity to the distressing nature of the attacks, appropriate responses to victims' most common concerns (e.g., possible escalation, removal of defamatory content), and instruction on documenting future attacks would be of great service to victims. Responding officers can provide written information to victims about relevant state and federal laws, strategies for bolstering digital security, nongovernmental organizations specializing in digital harassment, and platform policies. Best practices might also involve following up to see how the victim is doing and whether the attacks have subsided.

In cases where the abuse is particularly intense or ongoing, social workers and advocates would also be a valuable component of structured support. Typically, these kinds of assistance are provided when the person is a victim of a crime, but in cases where the harm is comparable, policymakers should not allow the legal obstacles women face in pursuing attackers to stand in the way of such services. Social workers can provide crisis intervention, emotional support, information about legal alternatives, guidance about talking with employers and families about the abuse, and referral services as needed. Meanwhile, trained advocates can help victims learn about their rights, review and implement digital security options as needed, assist them as they work with platforms and employers, answer questions about legal options, help with paperwork, and generally provide a sounding board. The harms of digital abuse are similar to those imposed by legally delineated crimes; even without a legal structure around prosecutable online harassment, the resources available to its victims should be similar, too.

Responsive and responsible platforms are also key to victim-centered support. Upon request, tech companies should be willing to commit to temporary, proactive moderation of content directed toward or referencing those who have been targeted by documented attacks (even if the attacks have thus far been contained to another platform). By proactive, I am not suggesting review prior to publication, which would be a major breach of existing protocols, but rather prompt review *upon* publication. Content deemed in violation would be diverted to a repository made available to the victim or law enforcement as needed. This is a modest, but meaningful measure. Platforms are asked only to ensure enforcement of their own rules, for a brief period, for at-risk users. Certainly, they are capable of doing far more to manage and deter digital hate; what I have proposed here is a minimal stop-gap measure that might minimize the harm coming to those already under fire.

Policymakers have been increasingly attentive to issues around digital abuse, as evinced in the flurry of new legislation targeting nonconsensual pornography. Creating, incentivizing, and funding victim-centered support structures is an important extension of these legislative efforts. As I reflect on the accounts women shared in which they felt lost and invisible, a sensitive and well-informed police officer, an expert to offer emotional support, and a platform willing to enforce its rules would have made a tremendous difference. I am less optimistic that these supports would ultimately be enough to prevent the democratic disturbances that stem from women's self-censorship and withdrawal.

Credible Threat

Attacks against women pose a credible threat to democracy. And that is a serious problem—for all of us. We need to hear the voices of White women and people of color, of queer women, of Jews and Muslims and atheists. We also need to have full information on all political issues, not just those that are uncontroversial. If female-identifying experts and journalists and bloggers are afraid to address sexual assault or immigration, we will not have a complete picture. We need women to be willing to run for office. We need activists like Emma Gonzalez, Malala Yousafzai, Tarana Burke, and Greta Thunberg to push us to decide what is and is not acceptable. To the extent we fail to solve the problems faced by the participants in this research, we fail to solve our own.

We need reform. We need structural solutions that will prevent and ameliorate patterned resistance to women's visibility, but this is no small feat. Perhaps that means breaking up big tech, so that competitors such as Mastodon, a platform on which users control their digital environment by choosing among varied servers, each with its own code of conduct and moderation policies, can be viable. Perhaps it means the end of publish-then-filter approaches to content moderation, perhaps it means holding platforms accountable for the most serious harms meted out on their terrain, and perhaps it means broadening the search for better hybrid solutions.

We must preserve the right to free expression for all. And, as uncomfortable and counterintuitive as it seems, this means that those hell bent on silencing others need to find something else to say. They should argue with ideas, challenge assumptions, and by all means question facts, but they need to take the rape threats and pornographic gifs off the table.

Until meaningful reform takes place, we must let it be known that women, especially women of color, are entering rough waters. Employers and managers who incentivize or require their staff to promote themselves or their work on social media or ask them to engage with constituents, clients, customers, or readers in online spaces must be aware that they are asking those staff to enter hostile environments. Similarly, before taking away elected officials' right to block people on social media, we need to think seriously about how such edicts reinforce existing social inequalities. President Donald Trump and Representative Alexandria Ocasio-Cortez (D-NY) have both faced lawsuits for blocking critics on Twitter, but the implications of their mandated openness is unquestionably shaped by their identities (Sobieraj et al. 2020). *Equal* treatment is not always *fair*. Those who have known only the luxury of a relatively comfortable digital life—such as *New York Times'* Bret Stephens, so outraged to have been called a "bedbug" on Twitter—may find the notion hard to fathom that these are often abusive spaces (Rupar 2019). But this hostility is now well documented, and we need to adjust our expectations, reward structures, and support systems accordingly.

Notes

Introduction

1. Other researchers may be interested in knowing the logistics of my interviews and analysis: I recruited participants through referrals, snowball sampling, and reaching out to women who have publicly referenced their own digital attacks or been referenced in reports of online harassment. I also recruited participants at the South by Southwest conference in Austin, Texas, and at the Netroots Nation conference in St. Louis, Missouri. Two participants were part of my existing social network. Through these efforts I found a remarkable number of women who had been targeted, though often they decided they did not wish to revisit those episodes. I am a White woman, and I suspect this contributed to the particular challenge I faced finding women of color who felt comfortable telling me their stories. The most elusive group proved to be those women who chose to leave digital publics altogether. While I spoke with a few of them, none were comfortable sharing their experiences even confidentially. One, for example, said she was opposed in principle to letting the abuse take even another second of her time or energy. Another has lost all confidence in data security and feared the interview audio or transcript could be hacked. When I offered to take notes instead, she said she was just too afraid. I respect their choices. Clearly, however, these missing voices are especially significant. In the end, the dataset is rich, but imperfect, as is often the case. I am deeply appreciative of the women who allowed me into their lives for these interviews.

   The vast majority of the interviews were conducted by phone or video conference. With permission, they were recorded for transcription purposes. The interviews ranged from 50 minutes to two hours long, with most lasting just over an hour. Data were coded using open coding with Dedoose qualitative analysis software.

2. Of course, the irony is that the same attributes—low cost, the ability to be anonymous if one chooses, and the limited oversight and regulation in many of these arenas—that render these platforms accessible to those from marginalized groups, also open the floodgates for those who may abuse them.

3. On these inequities see Benhabib (1996), Fraser (1990), Mansbridge (1990), and Young (2002).

4. Burrows (2010), Eckert and Chada (2013), Graham and Smith (2016), Gregory (1994), Jacobs (2000), Simone (2006), and Squires (2000) all provide illustrations.

5. This is not to suggest that marginalized views are necessarily pro-social. Jessie Daniels's (2009a) work on white supremacist groups online serves as one powerful example.

6. The suicides of young teens Rehtaeh Parsons and Audrie Potts, both of whom took their lives after being humiliated by digital images of their sexual assaults, stand out as examples from the headlines.

7. Too often intersectional differences are overlooked in research on women's experiences online (Hackworth 2018). I hope to have made some progress in this regard—the variation in women's digital lives will be visible as the participants in this research share their stories—but it is incomplete. And although distinctions between White women and women of color come into sharp relief, my sample size prevents me from drawing conclusions among the many subgroups of women. I hope future research, including my own, will be able to excavate these differences more meaningfully.

8. Digital life is, of course, rife with gender. Niles Van Doorn uses three case studies to show the way "online articulations of gender, sexuality, and embodiment are intricately woven with people's physical embeddings in everyday life, as well as in the new media technologies they employ" (2011, 532). The gendered body is often visible in digital publics through photos and videos, but gender remains a focal point even when it is not visually referenced. Research suggests that rather than using online spaces as a way to "change" or conceal our gender or racial identities, we use them to reach out to others, to seek affirmation, and to build relationships (Daniels 2009a). What's more, many of the most popular platforms build gender relevance into their architecture, requiring registrants to identify by gender. For example, Facebook requires that you choose a gender category (either male or female) when you register. Since 2013, members have been able to then change their gender to a custom option and choose a preferred pronoun. This more inclusive turn has broadened the range of options yet not reduced the salience of gender categorization (see Bevins 2003 for a discussion of misgendering on Facebook).

9. Interestingly, this dis-ease may not be necessary. Jenny Korn's (2015) work on Presumed Logic for Automatic Teaching Operations (PLATO) in the 1970s shows the way even "genderless" online spaces are rife with gender inequality.

Chapter 2

1. New York Times Co. v. Sullivan, 376 U.S. 254 (1964).

Conclusions

1. These issues are "alleged" because the terms of the settlement involved no admission of wrongdoing, but the company was cited for deceptive privacy settings, unauthorized third-party access to user data, misuse of user phone numbers shared for the purposes of account security, and misleading users about their facial recognition practices (Kelly 2019).

2. The amount of effort invested in developing the structure and parameters of the Oversight Board is impressive. See Facebook's report on the global feedback and input process for more information: https://about.fb.com/news/2019/06/global-feedback-on-oversight-board/.

Bibliography

Adams, Catherine. 2018. "'They Go for Gender First.'" *Journalism Practice* 12 (7): 850–69. https://doi.org/10.1080/17512786.2017.1350115.

Amnesty International. 2018. "Troll Patrol Report." *Amnesty International.* 2018. https://decoders.amnesty.org/projects/troll-patrol/findings.

Angelou, Maya. 1978. "Still I Rise." In *And Still I Rise: A Book of Poems.* New York: Random House.

Antunovic, Dunja. 2019. "'We Wouldn't Say It to Their Faces': Online Harassment, Women Sports Journalists, and Feminism." *Feminist Media Studies* 19 (3): 428–42.

Astor, Maggie. 2018. "For Female Candidates, Harassment and Threats Come Every Day." *New York Times*, August 24, 2018, sec. U.S. https://www.nytimes.com/2018/08/24/us/politics/women-harassment-elections.html.

Baker, Douglas D., David E. Terpstra, and Kinley Larntz. 1990. "The Influence of Individual Characteristics and Severity of Harassing Behavior on Reactions to Sexual Harassment." *Sex Roles* 22 (5): 305–25. https://doi.org/10.1007/BF00288336.

Barak, Azy. 2005. "Sexual Harassment on the Internet." *Social Science Computer Review* 23 (1): 77–92.

Bates, Samantha. 2017. "Revenge Porn and Mental Health: A Qualitative Analysis of the Mental Health Effects of Revenge Porn on Female Survivors." *Feminist Criminology* 12 (1): 22–42.

Bedera, Nicole, and Kristjane Nordmeyer. 2015. "'Never Go Out Alone': An Analysis of College Rape Prevention Tips." *Sexuality & Culture* 19 (3): 533–42. https://doi.org/10.1007/s12119-015-9274-5.

Benhabib, Seyla. 1996. *Democracy and Difference: Contesting the Boundaries of the Political.* Princeton, NJ: Princeton University Press.

Bennett, W. Lance, and Steven Livingston. 2018. "The Disinformation Order: Disruptive Communication and the Decline of Democratic Institutions." *European Journal of Communication* 33 (2): 122–39. https://doi.org/10.1177/0267323118760317.

Berdahl, Jennifer L. 2007. "The Sexual Harassment of Uppity Women." *Journal of Applied Psychology* 92 (2): 425–37. https://doi.org/10.1037/0021-9010.92.2.425.

Bevins, Rena. 2003. "The Gender Binary Will Not Be Deprogrammed: Ten Years of Coding Gender on Facebook." *New Media & Society* 19 (6): 880–98.

Bonilla, Yarimar, and Jonathan Rosa. 2015. "#Ferguson: Digital Protest, Hashtag Ethnography, and the Racial Politics of Social Media in the United States." *American Ethnologist* 42 (1): 4–17. https://doi.org/10.1111/amet.12112.

Bordia, Prashant. 1997. "Face-to-Face versus Computer-Mediated Communication: A Synthesis of the Experimental Literature." *Journal of Business Communication* 34 (1): 99–118. https://doi.org/10.1177/002194369703400106.

Boucher, Eliane M., Jeffrey T. Hancock, and Philip J. Dunham. 2008. "Interpersonal Sensitivity in Computer-Mediated and Face-to-Face Conversations." *Media Psychology 11* (2): 235–58.

Boulianne, Shelley, Karolina Koc-Michalska, and Bruce Bimber. 2020. "Mobilizing Media: Comparing TV and Social Media Effects on Protest Mobilization." *Information, Communication & Society*: 1–23. https://doi.org/10.1080/1369118X.2020.1713847.

Braidotti, Rosi. 2003. "Cyberfeminism with a Difference." In *Futures of Critical Theory: Dreams of Difference*, 239–59. Lanham, MD: Rowman & Littlefield.

Brenan, Megan. 2019. "Americans' Trust in Mass Media Edges Down to 41%." *Gallup.Com*. September 26, 2019. https://news.gallup.com/poll/267047/americans-trust-mass-media-edges-down.aspx.

Burrows, Elizabeth. 2010. "Tools of Resistance: The Roles of Two Indigenous Newspapers in Building an Indigenous Public Sphere." *Australian Journalism Review 32* (2): 33.

Chen, Gina Masullo, Paromita Pain, Victoria Y. Chen, Madlin Mekelburg, Nina Springer, and Franziska Troger. 2018. "'You Really Have to Have a Thick Skin': A Cross-Cultural Perspective on How Online Harassment Influences Female Journalists." *Journalism*, April, https://doi.org/10.1177/1464884918768500.

Chen, Rachel. 2019. "Facebook and Twitter Are Broken, But You Should Still Report Hate—VICE." *Vice Motherboard*, January 23, 2019. https://www.vice.com/en_us/article/d3mzqx/social-media-is-broken-but-you-should-still-report-hate.

Citron, Danielle Keats. 2009. "Cyber Civil Rights." *Boston University Law Review 89*: 61.

Citron, Danielle Keats. 2014. *Hate Crimes in Cyberspace*. Cambridge, MA: Harvard University Press.

Clark, Sheryl. 2015. "Running into Trouble: Constructions of Danger and Risk in Girls' Access to Outdoor Space and Physical Activity." *Sport, Education and Society 20* (8): 1012–28.

Claypool, Heather M., Diane M. Mackie, Teresa Garcia-Marques, Ashley McIntosh, and Ashton Udall. 2004. "The Effects of Personal Relevance and Repetition on Persuasive Processing." *Social Cognition 22* (3): 310–35. https://doi.org/10.1521/soco.22.3.310.35970.

Cortina, Lilia M., and S. Arzu Wasti. 2005. "Profiles in Coping: Responses to Sexual Harassment across Persons, Organizations, and Cultures." *Journal of Applied Psychology 90* (1): 182–92. https://doi.org/10.1037/0021-9010.90.1.182.

Crenshaw, Kimberle. 1989. "Demarginalizing the Intersection of Race and Sex: A Black Feminist Critique of Antidiscrimination Doctrine, Feminist Theory and Antiracist Politics." *University of Chicago Legal Forum*, vol. 1989: *Feminism in the Law: Theory, Practice, and Criticism*, 139–68.

Cuen, Leigh, and Jishai Evers. 2016. "All of the Sexist Slurs Trump Supporters Use to Attack Megyn Kelly." *Vocativ*, January 27. https://www.vocativ.com/276256/donald-trump-megyn-kelly/.

"Cyber Crime." n.d. Folder. Federal Bureau of Investigation. Accessed February 8, 2020. https://www.fbi.gov/investigate/cyber.

Daniels, Jessie. 2009a. *Cyber Racism: White Supremacy Online and the New Attack on Civil Rights*. https://rowman.com/ISBN/9780742561571.

Daniels, Jessie. 2009b. "Rethinking Cyberfeminism(s): Race, Gender, and Embodiment." *Women's Studies Quarterly 37* (1/2): 101–24.

Denissen, Amy M. 2010. "Crossing the Line: How Women in the Building Trades Interpret and Respond to Sexual Conduct at Work." *Journal of Contemporary Ethnography 39* (3): 297–327. https://doi.org/10.1177/0891241609341827.

Department of Infrastructure, Transport. 2019. "Consultation on a New Online Safety Act." *Text*. December 10. https://www.communications.gov.au/have-your-say/consultation-new-online-safety-act.

"Despite YouTube Policy Update, Anti-Semitic, White Supremacist Channels Remain." 2019. Anti-Defamation League. https://www.adl.org/blog/despite-youtube-policy-update-anti-semitic-white-supremacist-channels-remain.

Dignam, Pierce Alexander, and Deana A. Rohlinger. 2019. "Misogynistic Men Online: How the Red Pill Helped Elect Trump." *Signs: Journal of Women in Culture and Society 44* (3): 589–612. https://doi.org/10.1086/701155.

Doorn, Niels van. 2011. "Digital Spaces, Material Traces: How Matter Comes to Matter in Online Performances of Gender, Sexuality and Embodiment." *Media, Culture & Society 33* (4): 531–47. https://doi.org/10.1177/0163443711398692.

Doquir, Pierre François. 2019. "The Social Media Council: Bringing Human Rights Standards to Content Moderation on Social Media." *Models for Platform Governance.* Centre for International Governance Innovation. https://www.cigionline.org/articles/social-media-council-bringing-human-rights-standards-content-moderation-social-media.

Döring, Nicola, and M. Rohangis Mohseni. 2018. "Male Dominance and Sexism on YouTube: Results of Three Content Analyses." *Feminist Media Studies 19* (4): 512–24.

Dresden, Brooke E., Alexander Y. Dresden, Robert D. Ridge, and Niwako Yamawaki. 2018. "No Girls Allowed: Women in Male-Dominated Majors Experience Increased Gender Harassment and Bias." *Psychological Reports 21* (3): 459–74. https://doi.org/10.1177/0033294117730357.

Dubrovsky, Vitaly J., Sara Kiesler, and Beheruz N. Sethna. 1991. "The Equalization Phenomenon: Status Effects in Computer-Mediated and Face-to-Face Decision-Making Groups." *Human–Computer Interaction 6* (2): 119–46. https://doi.org/10.1207/s15327051hci0602_2.

Earl, Jennifer, and Katrina Kimport. 2011. *Digitally Enabled Social Change: Activism in the Internet Age.* Cambridge, MA: MIT Press.

Eckert, Stine. 2018. "Fighting for Recognition: Online Abuse of Women Bloggers in Germany, Switzerland, the United Kingdom, and the United States." *New Media & Society 20* (4): 1282–302.

Eckert, Stine, and Kalyani Chadha. 2013. "Muslim Bloggers in Germany: An Emerging Counterpublic." *Media, Culture & Society 35* (8): 926–42. https://doi.org/10.1177/0163443713501930.

"Equality and Hate Speech." n.d. *ARTICLE 19.* Accessed February 9, 2020. https://www.article19.org/issue/equality-and-hate-speech/.

"The EU Code of Conduct on Countering Illegal Hate Speech Online." 2016. Text. European Commission. https://ec.europa.eu/info/policies/justice-and-fundamental-rights/combatting-discrimination/racism-and-xenophobia/eu-code-conduct-countering-illegal-hate-speech-online_en.

Everbach, Tracy. 2018. "'I Realized It Was about Them . . . Not Me': Women Sports Journalists and Harassment." In *Mediating Misogyny: Gender, Technology, and Harassment,* edited by Jacqueline Ryan Vickery and Tracy Everbach, 131–49. Cham, Switzerland: Springer International. https://doi.org/10.1007/978-3-319-72917-6_7.

Ezzy, Douglas. 1998. "Theorizing Narrative Identity:" *Sociological Quarterly 39* (2): 239–52. https://doi.org/10.1111/j.1533-8525.1998.tb00502.x.

"Facebook Transparency Report: Community Standards Enforcement." 2019. https://transparency.facebook.com/community-standards-enforcement.

Fagone, Jason. 2016. "The Serial Swatter." *New York Times Magazine,* November 24. https://www.nytimes.com/2015/11/29/magazine/the-serial-swatter.html.

Fairchild, Kimberly, and Laurie A. Rudman. 2008. "Everyday Stranger Harassment and Women's Objectification." *Social Justice Research 21* (3): 338–57. https://doi.org/10.1007/s11211-008-0073-0.

Farrell, Tracie, Miriam Fernandez, Jakub Novotny, and Harith Alani. 2019. "Exploring Misogyny across the Manosphere in Reddit." In *Proceedings of the 10th ACM Conference on Web Science,* 87–96. WebSci '19. Boston, MA, USA: Association for Computing Machinery. https://doi.org/10.1145/3292522.3326045.

Fazio, Lisa K., David G. Rand, and Gordon Pennycook. 2019. "Repetition Increases Perceived Truth Equally for Plausible and Implausible Statements." *Psychonomic Bulletin & Review* 26 (5): 1705–10. https://doi.org/10.3758/s13423-019-01651-4.

Fenton, Natalie. 2019. "(Dis)Trust." *Journalism* 20 (1): 36–39. https://doi.org/10.1177/1464884918807068.

Ferber, Abby L. 2018. "'Are You Willing to Die for This Work?' Public Targeted Online Harassment in Higher Education: SWS Presidential Address." *Gender & Society* 32 (3): 301–20. https://doi.org/10.1177/0891243218766831.

Fileborn, Bianca. 2016. "Doing Gender, Doing Safety? Young Adults' Production of Safety on a Night Out." *Gender, Place & Culture* 23 (8): 1107–20. https://doi.org/10.1080/0966369X.2015.1090413.

Filipovic, Jill. 2007. "Blogging While Female: How Internet Misogyny Parallels Real-World Harassment Responding to Internet Harassment." *Yale Journal of Law and Feminism* 19 (1): 295–304.

Finn, Jerry. 2004. "A Survey of Online Harassment at a University Campus." *Journal of Interpersonal Violence* 19 (4): 468–83. https://doi.org/10.1177/0886260503262083.

Fisher, Dana R. 2019. *American Resistance: From the Women's March to the Blue Wave*. New York: Columbia University Press.

Foster, Jeffrey L., Thomas Huthwaite, Julia A. Yesberg, Maryanne Garry, and Elizabeth F. Loftus. 2012. "Repetition, Not Number of Sources, Increases Both Susceptibility to Misinformation and Confidence in the Accuracy of Eyewitnesses." *Acta Psychologica* 139 (2): 320–26. https://doi.org/10.1016/j.actpsy.2011.12.004.

Fox, Jesse, and Wai Yen Tang. 2017. "Women's Experiences with General and Sexual Harassment in Online Video Games: Rumination, Organizational Responsiveness, Withdrawal, and Coping Strategies." *New Media & Society* 19 (8): 1290–307. https://doi.org/10.1177/1461444816635778.

"France Online Hate Speech Law to Force Social Media Sites to Act Quickly." 2019. *The Guardian*. July 9, sec. World news. https://www.theguardian.com/world/2019/jul/09/france-online-hate-speech-law-social-media.

Franks, Mary Anne. 2017. "Revenge Porn Reform: A View from the Front Lines." *Florida Law Review* 69 (5): 1251–338.

Franks, Mary Anne. 2011. "Sexual Harassment 2.0 Special Feature: Cyberlaw." *Maryland Law Review* 71 (3): 655–704.

Fraser, Nancy. 1990. "Rethinking the Public Sphere: A Contribution to the Critique of Actually Existing Democracy." *Social Text* 25/26: 56–80.

Frazier, Kathryn E., and Rachel Joffe Falmagne. 2014. "Empowered Victims? Women's Contradictory Positions in the Discourse of Violence Prevention:" *Feminism & Psychology*, October. https://doi.org/10.1177/0959353514552036.

Freelon, Deen, Charlton McIlwain, and Meredith Clark. 2018. "Quantifying the Power and Consequences of Social Media Protest." *New Media & Society* 20 (3): 990–1011. https://doi.org/10.1177/1461444816676646.

Garde-Hansen, Joanne, and Kristyn Gorton. 2013. *Emotion Online: Theorizing Affect on the Internet*. London: Palgrave Macmillan. https://doi.org/10.1057/9781137312877.

Gardiner, Becky. 2018. "'It's a Terrible Way to Go to Work:' What 70 Million Readers' Comments on the Guardian Revealed about Hostility to Women and Minorities Online." *Feminist Media Studies* 18 (4): 592–608. https://doi.org/10.1080/14680777.2018.1447334.

George, Joey F., George K. Easton, J. F. Nunamaker, and Gregory B. Northcraft. 1990. "A Study of Collaborative Group Work with and without Computer-Based Support." *Information Systems Research* 1 (4): 394–415. https://doi.org/10.1287/isre.1.4.394.

Gidron, Noam, James Adams, and Will Horne. 2019. "Toward a Comparative Research Agenda on Affective Polarization in Mass Publics." *APSA Comparative Politics Newsletter* 29 (1): 30–36.

Gillespie, Tarleton. 2018b. *Custodians of the Internet: Platforms, Content Moderation, and the Hidden Decisions That Shape Social Media.* New Haven, CT: Yale University Press.

Gillespie, Tarleton. 2018a. "Platforms Are Not Intermediaries." *Georgetown Law and Technology Review 2* (2): 190–216.

Goffman, Erving. 1959. *The Presentation of Self in Everyday Life.* New York: Anchor.

Gorwa, Robert. 2019. "The Shifting Definition of Platform Governance." Models for Platform Governance. Centre for International Governance Innovation. https://www.cigionline. org/articles/shifting-definition-platform-governance.

Graham, Kathryn, Sharon Bernards, Antonia Abbey, Tara M. Dumas, and Samantha Wells. 2017. "When Women Do Not Want It: Young Female Bargoers' Experiences with and Responses to Sexual Harassment in Social Drinking Contexts." *Violence against Women 23* (12): 1419–41. https://doi.org/10.1177/1077801216661037.

Graham, Roderick, and Shawn Smith. 2016. "The Content of Our #Characters: Black Twitter as Counterpublic." *Sociology of Race and Ethnicity 2* (4): 433–49. https://doi.org/10.1177/2332649216639067.

Gray, Kishonna L. 2012. "Intersecting Oppressions and Online Communities: Examining the Experiences of Women of Color in Xbox Live." *Information, Communication & Society 15* (3): 411–28.

Gray, Kishonna L. 2014. *Race, Gender, and Deviance in Xbox Live: Theoretical Perspectives from the Virtual Margins.* New York: Routledge.

Gregory, Steven. 1994. "Race, Identity and Political Activism: The Shifting Contours of the African American Public Sphere." *Public Culture 7* (1): 147–64. https://doi.org/10.1215/08992363-7-1-147.

Habermas, Jürgen. 1991. *The Structural Transformation of the Public Sphere: An Inquiry into a Category of Bourgeois Society.* 6th ed.. Cambridge, MA: MIT Press.

Hackworth, Lucy. 2018. "Limitations of 'Just Gender': The Need for an Intersectional Reframing of Online Harassment Discourse and Research." In *Mediating Misogyny: Gender, Technology, and Harassment,* edited by Jacqueline Ryan Vickery and Tracy Everbach, 51–70. Cham, Switzerland: Springer International. https://doi.org/10.1007/978-3-319-72917-6_3.

Haraway, Donna. 1987. "A Manifesto for Cyborgs: Science, Technology, and Socialist Feminism in the 1980s." *Australian Feminist Studies 2* (4): 1–42. https://doi.org/10.1080/08164649.1987.9961538.

Harlow, Summer. 2012. "Social Media and Social Movements: Facebook and an Online Guatemalan Justice Movement That Moved Offline." *New Media & Society 14* (2): 225–43. https://doi.org/10.1177/1461444811410408.

Harris-Perry, Melissa V. 2011. *Sister Citizen: Shame, Stereotypes, and Black Women in America.* New Haven, CT: Yale University Press.

Harvey, Del. 2014. *Protecting Twitter Users (Sometimes from Themselves).* TED Talks. https://www.ted.com/talks/del_harvey_protecting_twitter_users_sometimes_from_themselves.

Haskell, Rob. 2018. "Serena Williams on Motherhood, Marriage, and Making Her Comeback." *Vogue,* January. https://www.vogue.com/article/serena-williams-vogue-cover-interview-february-2018.

Henry, Nicola, and Anastasia Powell. 2015. "Embodied Harms: Gender, Shame, and Technology-Facilitated Sexual Violence." *Violence against Women,* March. https://doi.org/10.1177/1077801215576581.

Herring, Susan C. 1996. *Computer-Mediated Communication.* Amsterdam: John Benjamins. https://benjamins.com/catalog/pbns.39.

Herring, Susan C. 2002. "Computer-Mediated Communication on the Internet." *Annual Review of Information Science and Technology 36* (1): 109–68. https://doi.org/10.1002/aris.1440360104.

Herring, Susan C. 1999. "The Rhetorical Dynamics of Gender Harassment On-Line." *Information Society 15* (3): 151–67.

Herring, Susan C., Kirk Job-Sluder, Rebecca Scheckler, and Sasha Barab. 2002. "Searching for Safety Online: Managing 'Trolling' in a Feminist Forum." *Information Society 18* (October): 371–84. https://doi.org/10.1080/01972240290108186.

Hochschild, Arlie Russell. 1979. "Emotion Work, Feeling Rules, and Social Structure." *American Journal of Sociology 85* (3): 551–75. https://doi.org/10.1086/227049.

Holland, Kathryn J., and Lilia M. Cortina. 2013. "When Sexism and Feminism Collide: The Sexual Harassment of Feminist Working Women." *Psychology of Women Quarterly*, April. https://doi.org/10.1177/0361684313482873.

Hollander, Jocelyn A. 2001. "Vulnerability and Dangerousness: The Construction of Gender through Conversation about Violence." *Gender and Society 15* (1): 83–109.

Hughes, Karen D., and Vela Tadic. 1998. "'Something to Deal With': Customer Sexual Harassment and Women's Retail Service Work in Canada." *Gender, Work & Organization 5* (4): 207–19. https://doi.org/10.1111/1468-0432.00058.

"Internet Crime Complaint Center (IC3)." n.d. Accessed February 8, 2020. https://www.ic3.gov/default.aspx.

Isaac, Mike, and Cecilia Kang. 2019. "F.T.C. Is Said to Consider an Injunction against Facebook." *New York Times*, December 12, 2019, sec. Technology. https://www.nytimes.com/2019/12/12/technology/ftc-facebook-injunction.html.

Iyengar, Shanto, Yphtach Lelkes, Matthew Levendusky, Neil Malhotra, and Sean J. Westwood. 2019. "The Origins and Consequences of Affective Polarization in the United States." *Annual Review of Political Science 22* (1): 129–46. https://doi.org/10.1146/annurev-polisci-051117-073034.

Iyengar, Shanto, and Sean J. Westwood. 2015. "Fear and Loathing across Party Lines: New Evidence on Group Polarization." *American Journal of Political Science 59* (3): 690–707. https://doi.org/10.1111/ajps.12152.

Jacobs, Ronald N. 2000. *Race, Media, and the Crisis of Civil Society: From Watts to Rodney King.* Cambridge: Cambridge University Press.

Jane, Emma A. 2014a. "'Back to the Kitchen, Cunt': Speaking the Unspeakable about Online Misogyny." *Continuum 28* (4): 558–70. https://doi.org/10.1080/10304312.2014.924479.

Jane, Emma A. 2018. "Systemic Misogyny Exposed: Translating Rapeglish from the Manosphere with a Random Rape Threat Generator." *International Journal of Cultural Studies 21* (6): 661–80. https://doi.org/10.1177/1367877917734042.

Jane, Emma A. 2014b. "'Your a Ugly, Whorish, Slut.'" *Feminist Media Studies 14* (4): 531–46. https://doi.org/10.1080/14680777.2012.741073.

Jubainville, Hugo d'Arbois de, and Camille Vanier. 2017. "Women's Avoidance Behaviours in Public Transport in the Ile-de-France Region." *Crime Prevention and Community Safety 19* (3): 183–98. https://doi.org/10.1057/s41300-017-0023-6.

Jurgenson, Nathan. 2011. "Digital Dualism and the Fallacy of Web Objectivity." *Cyborgology (blog)*. September 13, 2011. https://thesocietypages.org/cyborgology/2011/09/13/digital-dualism-and-the-fallacy-of-web-objectivity/.

Jurgenson, Nathan. 2012. "When Atoms Meet Bits: Social Media, the Mobile Web and Augmented Revolution." *Future Internet 4* (1): 83–91. .

Kabat-Farr, Dana, and Lilia M. Cortina. 2014. "Sex-Based Harassment in Employment: New Insights into Gender and Context." *Law and Human Behavior 38* (1): 58–72. https://doi.org/10.1037/lhb0000045.

Kash, Gwen. 2019. "Always on the Defensive: The Effects of Transit Sexual Assault on Travel Behavior and Experience in Colombia and Bolivia." *Journal of Transport & Health 13* (June): 234–46. https://doi.org/10.1016/j.jth.2019.04.004.

Keats Citron, Danielle. 2018. "Extremist Speech, Compelled Conformity, and Censorship Creep." *Notre Dame Law Review 93* (3): 1035–71.

Keller, Jessalynn Marie. 2012. "Virtual Feminisms." *Information, Communication & Society 15* (3): 429–47. https://doi.org/10.1080/1369118X.2011.642890.

Kelly, Makena. 2019. "Why Wasn't the FTC Harder on Facebook?" *The Verge*, July 25. https://www.theverge.com/2019/7/25/8930630/facebook-ftc-settlement-privacy-cambridge-analytica-congress.

Kendall, Lori. 2002. *Hanging Out in the Virtual Pub.* Berkeley: University of California Press.

Kerr, Sarah Stein, Ainara Tiefenthaler, and Nicole Fineman. 2018. *"Where's Your Husband?"* What Female Candidates Hear on the Trail. *New York Times Video.* https://www.nytimes.com/video/us/politics/100000006027375/women-politics-harassment.html.

Klonick, Kate. 2018. "Does Facebook's Oversight Board Finally Solve the Problem of Online Speech?" Models for Platform Governance. Centre of International Governance Innovation. https://georgetownlawtechreview.org/wp-content/uploads/2018/07/2.2-Gilespie-pp-198-216.pdf.

Konik, Julie, and Lilia M. Cortina. 2008. "Policing Gender at Work: Intersections of Harassment Based on Sex and Sexuality." *Social Justice Research 21* (3): 313–37. https://doi.org/10.1007/s11211-008-0074-z.

Korn, Jenny Ungbha. 2015. "'Genderless' Online Discourse in the 1970s: Muted Group Theory in Early Social Computing." In *Ada's Legacy: Cultures of Computing from the Victorian to the Digital Age*, edited by Robin Hammerman and Andrew L. Russell, 213–30. Williston, VT: Morgan & Claypool.

Larsen, M.-L., M. Hilden, and Ø Lidegaard. 2015. "Sexual Assault: A Descriptive Study of 2500 Female Victims over a 10-Year Period." *BJOG: An International Journal of Obstetrics & Gynaecology 122* (4): 577–84. https://doi.org/10.1111/1471-0528.13093.

Lazarus, Richard S., and Susan Folkman. 1984. *Stress, Appraisal, and Coping.* New York: Springer.

Lenhart, Amanda, Michele Ybarra, Kathryn Zickhur, and Myeshia Price-Feeney. 2016. "Online Harassment, Digital Abuse, and Cyberstalking in America." *Data & Society Research Institute.* https://www.datasociety.net/pubs/oh/Online_Harassment_2016.pdf.

Levey, Tania G. 2018. *Sexual Harassment Online: Shaming and Silencing Women in the Digital Age.* Boulder, CO: Lynne Rienner.

Lockhart, P. R. 2018. "What Serena Williams's Scary Childbirth Story Says about Medical Treatment of Black Women." Vox, January 11. https://www.vox.com/identities/2018/1/11/16879984/serena-williams-childbirth-scare-black-women.

Loukaitou-Sideris, Anastasia. 2014. "Fear and Safety in Transit Environments from the Women's Perspective." *Security Journal 27* (2): 242–56. https://doi.org/10.1057/sj.2014.9.

Maass, Anne, Mara Cadinu, Gaia Guarnieri, and Annalisa Grasselli. 2003. "Sexual Harassment under Social Identity Threat: The Computer Harassment Paradigm." *Journal of Personality and Social Psychology 85* (5): 853–70. https://doi.org/10.1037/0022-3514.85.5.853.

MacAllister, Julia M. 2016. "The Doxing Dilemma: Seeking a Remedy for the Malicious Publication of Personal Information Notes." *Fordham Law Review 85* (5): 2451–84.

Madden, Stephanie, Melissa Janoske, Rowena Briones Winkler, and Amanda Nell Edgar. 2018. "Mediated Misogynoir: Intersecting Race and Gender in Online Harassment." In *Mediating Misogyny: Gender, Technology, and Harassment*, edited by Jacqueline Ryan Vickery and Tracy Everbach, 71–90. Cham, Switzerland: Springer International. https://doi.org/10.1007/978-3-319-72917-6_4.

Madrigal, Alexis. 2018. "Inside Facebook's Fast-Growing Content-Moderation Effort." *The Atlantic*, February 7. https://www.theatlantic.com/technology/archive/2018/02/what-facebook-told-insiders-about-how-it-moderates-posts/552632/.

Magley, Vicki J., Craig R. Waldo, Fritz Drasgow, and Louise F. Fitzgerald. 1999. "The Impact of Sexual Harassment on Military Personnel: Is It the Same for Men and Women?" *Military Psychology 11* (3): 283–302. https://doi.org/10.1207/s15327876mp1103_5.

Mansbridge, Jane. 1990. "Self-Interest in Political Life." *Political Theory 18* (1): 132–53.

Mantilla, Karla. 2015. *Gendertrolling: How Misogyny Went Viral.* Santa Barbara, CA: Praeger.

Martin, James S., Christian A. Vaccaro, D. Alex Heckert, and Robert Heasley. 2015. "Epic Glory and Manhood Acts in Fantasy Role-Playing: Dagorhir as a Case Study." *Journal of Men's Studies* 23 (3): 293–314. https://doi.org/10.1177/1060826515601355.

Martin, Nina, and Renee Montagne. 2017. "Nothing Protects Black Women from Dying in Pregnancy and Childbirth." *ProPublica*, December 7. https://www.propublica.org/article/nothing-protects-black-women-from-dying-in-pregnancy-and-childbirth.

Massanari, Adrienne. 2017. "#Gamergate and the Fappening: How Reddit's Algorithm, Governance, and Culture Support Toxic Technocultures." *New Media & Society* 19 (3): 329–46. https://doi.org/10.1177/1461444815608807.

McCoy, Jennifer, Tahmina Rahman, and Murat Somer. 2018. "Polarization and the Global Crisis of Democracy: Common Patterns, Dynamics, and Pernicious Consequences for Democratic Polities." *American Behavioral Scientist* 62 (1): 16–42. https://doi.org/10.1177/0002764218759576.

McLaughlin, Heather, Christopher Uggen, and Amy Blackstone. 2012. "Sexual Harassment, Workplace Authority, and the Paradox of Power." *American Sociological Review* 77 (4): 625–47. https://doi.org/10.1177/0003122412451728.

McNay, Lois. 2004. "Agency and Experience: Gender as a Lived Relation." *Sociological Review* 52 (2_suppl): 175–90. https://doi.org/10.1111/j.1467-954X.2005.00530.x.

Meyer, Doug, and Eric Anthony Grollman. 2014. "Sexual Orientation and Fear at Night: Gender Differences among Sexual Minorities and Heterosexuals." *Journal of Homosexuality* 61 (4): 453–70. https://doi.org/10.1080/00918369.2013.834212.

Miller, Jody. 2008. *Getting Played: African American Girls, Urban Inequality, and Gendered Violence.* New York: New York University Press.

Mills, C. Wright. 1959. *The Sociological Imagination.* 40th Anniversary Edition. New York: Oxford University Press.

Milner, Ryan. 2012. "Hacking the Social: Internet Memes, Identity Antagonism, and the Logic of Lulz." *Fibreculture Journal* 22: 61–91.

Moniuszko, Sara M. 2019. "Joy Villa Faces Backlash, 'Sheer Hatred' over 'Build the Wall' Grammys Dress." *USA TODAY*, February 10. https://www.usatoday.com/story/life/entertainthis/2019/02/10/grammys-2019-red-carpet-gets-political-border-wall-inspired-dress/2832427002/.

Mutz, Diana C. 2002a. "The Consequences of Cross-Cutting Networks for Political Participation." *American Journal of Political Science* 46 (4): 838–55. https://doi.org/10.2307/3088437.

Mutz, Diana C. 2002b. "Cross-Cutting Social Networks: Testing Democratic Theory in Practice." *American Political Science Review* 96 (1): 111–26. https://doi.org/10.1017/S0003055402004264.

Nam, Taewoo. 2012. "Dual Effects of the Internet on Political Activism: Reinforcing and Mobilizing." *Government Information Quarterly* 29 (1): S90–97.

Newman, Nic, and Richard Fletcher. 2017. "Bias, Bullshit and Lies: Audience Perspectives on Low Trust in the Media." *Reuters Institute for the Study of Journalism.* https://papers.ssrn.com/sol3/papers.cfm?abstract_id=3173579.

Nielsen, Laura Beth. 2004. *License to Harass: Law, Hierarchy, and Offensive Public Speech.* Princeton, NJ: Princeton University Press. https://press.princeton.edu/books/paperback/9780691126104/license-to-harass.

"Nigeria Is Considering Incredibly Harsh Punishments for Social Media Users Who Criticize the Government." 2019. *Amnesty International.* December 4. https://www.amnesty.org/en/latest/news/2019/12/nigeria-bills-on-hate-speech-and-social-media-are-dangerous-attacks-on-freedom-of-expression/.

Norris, Pippa. 2001. *Digital Divide: Civic Engagement, Information Poverty, and the Internet Worldwide.* Cambridge: Cambridge University Press. https://doi.org/10.1017/CBO9781139164887.

Olson, Candi S. Carter, and Victoria LaPoe. 2017. "'Feminazis,' 'Libtards,' 'Snowflakes,' and 'Racists': Trolling and the Spiral of Silence Effect in Women, LGBTQIA Communities, and Disability Populations before and after the 2016 Election." *Journal of Public Interest Communications* 1 (2): 116–132. https://doi.org/10.32473/jpic.v1.i2.p116.

Ortiz-Espina, Esteban. 2019. "The Rise of Social Media." *Our World in Data.* https://ourworld-indata.org/rise-of-social-media.

Owen, Taylor. 2019. "Introduction: Why Platform Governance?" Models for Platform Governance. Centre for International Governance Innovation. https://www.cigionline.org/articles/introduction-why-platform-governance.

Papacharissi, Zizi. 2016. "Democracy Online: Civility, Politeness, and the Democratic Potential of Online Political Discussion Groups." *New Media & Society,* June. https://doi.org/10.1177/1461444804041444.

Park, Yong Jin. 2013. "Offline Status, Online Status: Reproduction of Social Categories in Personal Information Skill and Knowledge." *Social Science Computer Review 31* (6): 680–702. https://doi.org/10.1177/0894439313485202.

Patchin, Justin W., and Sameer Hinduja. 2006. "Bullies Move beyond the Schoolyard: A Preliminary Look at Cyberbullying." *Youth Violence and Juvenile Justice 4* (2): 148–69. https://doi.org/10.1177/1541204006286288.

Pearlin, Leonard I., and Carmi Schooler. 1978. "The Structure of Coping." *Journal of Health and Social Behavior 19* (1): 2–21. https://doi.org/10.2307/2136319.

Pennycook, Gordon, Tyrone D. Cannon, and David G. Rand. 2018. "Prior Exposure Increases Perceived Accuracy of Fake News." *Journal of Experimental Psychology: General 147* (12): 1865–80. https://doi.org/10.1037/xge0000465.

Phillips, Whitney. 2015. *This Is Why We Can't Have Nice Things: Mapping the Relationship between Online Trolling and Mainstream Culture.* Cambridge, MA: MIT Press.

Pintak, Lawrence, Jonathan Albright, Brian J. Bowe, and Shaheen Pasha. 2019. "#Islamophobia: Stoking Fear and Prejudice in the 2018 Midterms." *Social Science Research Council.* https://www.ssrc.org/publications/view/islamophobia-stoking-fear-and-prejudice-in-the-2018-midterms/.

Plant, Sadie. 1997. *Zeros and Ones.* London: Fourth Estate.

"Pregnancy Mortality Surveillance System." 2020. *Centers for Disease Control and Prevention.* February 4, 2020. https://www.cdc.gov/reproductivehealth/maternal-mortality/pregnancy-mortality-surveillance-system.htm.

"Proving Fault: Actual Malice and Negligence." n.d. *Digital Media Law Project.* Accessed January 26, 2020. http://www.dmlp.org/legal-guide/proving-fault-actual-malice-and-negligence.

RAINN. 2017. "Perpetrators of Sexual Violence: Statistics." *RAINN.* https://www.rainn.org/statistics/perpetrators-sexual-violence.

Rapp, Laura, Deeanna M. Button, Benjamin Fleury-Steiner, and Ruth Fleury-Steiner. 2010. "The Internet as a Tool for Black Feminist Activism: Lessons from an Online Antirape Protest." *Feminist Criminology,* August. https://doi.org/10.1177/1557085110371634.

Reagle, Joseph M. 2013. "'Free as in Sexist?' Free Culture and the Gender Gap." *First Monday 18* (1). https://doi.org/10.5210/fm.v18i1.4291.

Reagle, Joseph M. 2015. *Reading the Comments: Likers, Haters, and Manipulators at the Bottom of the Web.* Cambridge, MA: MIT Press.

Reinstein, Julia. 2018. "Black Women Are Speaking Out after Serena Williams Revealed She Faced Life-Threatening Birth Complications." *BuzzFeed News,* January 11. https://www.buzzfeednews.com/article/juliareinstein/serena-williams-birth-complications.

Rheault, Ludovic, Erica Rayment, and Andreea Musulan. 2019. "Politicians in the Line of Fire: Incivility and the Treatment of Women on Social Media." *Research & Politics 6* (1): 1–7. https://doi.org/10.1177/2053168018816228.

Riger, Stephanie, and Margaret T. Gordon. 1981. "The Fear of Rape: A Study in Social Control." *Journal of Social Issues 37* (4): 71–92. https://doi.org/10.1111/j.1540-4560.1981.tb01071.x.

Robison, Joshua, and Rachel L. Moskowitz. 2019. "The Group Basis of Partisan Affective Polarization." *Journal of Politics 81* (3): 1075–79. https://doi.org/10.1086/703069.

Rohlinger, Deana A., and Leslie Bunnage. 2017. "Did the Tea Party Movement Fuel the Trump-Train? The Role of Social Media in Activist Persistence and Political Change in the 21st Century." *Social Media + Society*: 1–11.

Romm, Tony. 2019. "Attorney General Barr Says DOJ Is Rethinking Law That Protects Tech Companies from Liability." *Washington Post*, December 10. https://www.washingtonpost.com/technology/2019/12/10/attorney-general-barr-takes-aim-tech-signaling-broad-doj-review-antitrust-privacy-speech/.

Roper, Emily A. 2016. "Concerns for Personal Safety among Female Recreational Runners." *Women in Sport and Physical Activity Journal 24* (2): 91–98. https://doi.org/10.1123/wspaj.2015-0013.

Rupar, Aaron. 2019. "Bret Stephens's 'Bedbug' Meltdown, Explained." *Vox*, August 27. https://www.vox.com/2019/8/27/20834957/bret-stephens-bedbug-meltdown-dave-karpf-new-york-times-explained.

Schradie, Jen. 2011. "The Digital Production Gap: The Digital Divide and Web 2.0 Collide." *Poetics 39* (2): 145–68.

Schradie, Jen. 2012. "The Trend of Class, Race, and Ethnicity in Social Media Inequality: Who Still Cannot Afford to Blog?" *Information, Communication & Society 15* (4): 555–71.

Schradie, Jen. 2015. "The Gendered Digital Production Gap: Inequalities of Affluence." *Communication and Information Technologies Annual 9*: 185–213.

Scott, Jennifer. 2019. "Women MPs Say Abuse Forcing Them from Politics." *BBC News*, October 31, 2019, sec. Election 2019. https://www.bbc.com/news/election-2019-50246969.

Scott, Mark, and Janosch Delcker. 2019. "Germany Lays Down Marker for Online Hate Speech Laws." *Politico*, 2019. https://www.politico.eu/article/germany-hate-speech-netzdg-angela-merkel-facebook-germany-twitter/.

"Sen. Harris Introduces Bill Aimed at Reducing Racial Disparities in Maternal Mortality." 2018. August 22. https://www.harris.senate.gov/news/press-releases/sen-harris-introduces-bill-aimed-at-reducing-racial-disparities-in-maternal-mortality.

Shepard, Ryan Michael. 2011. "Deeds Done in Different Words: A Genre-Based Approach to Third Party Presidential Campaign Discourse," May. https://kuscholarworks.ku.edu/handle/1808/8202.

Shepherd, Tamara, Alison Harvey, Tim Jordan, Sam Srauy, and Kate Miltner. 2015. "Histories of Hating." *Social Media + Society 1* (2): 1–10. https://doi.org/10.1177/2056305115603997.

Shirky, Clay. 2008. *Here Comes Everybody: The Power of Organizing without Organizations*. New York: Penguin Press.

Siebler, Frank, Saskia Sabelus, and Gerd Bohner. 2008. "A Refined Computer Harassment Paradigm: Validation, and Test of Hypotheses about Target Characteristics." *Psychology of Women Quarterly 32* (1): 22–35. https://doi.org/10.1111/j.1471-6402.2007.00404.x.

Siegel, Reva B. 2003. "A Short History of Sexual Harassment." In *Directions in Sexual Harassment Law 1*:1–39. New Haven, CT: Yale University Press.

Sills, Sophie, Chelsea Pickens, Karishma Beach, Lloyd Jones, Octavia Calder-Dawe, Paulette Benton-Greig, and Nicola Gavey. 2016. "Rape Culture and Social Media: Young Critics and a Feminist Counterpublic." *Feminist Media Studies 16* (6): 935–51. https://doi.org/10.1080/14680777.2015.1137962.

Silva, Luciana, and David Wright. 2009. "Safety Rituals: How Women Cope with the Fear of Sexual Violence." *Qualitative Report 14* (4): 746–72.

Simone, Maria. 2006. "CODEPINK Alert: Mediated Citizenship in the Public Sphere." *Social Semiotics 16* (2): 345–64. https://doi.org/10.1080/10350330600664904.

Slonje, Robert, and Peter K. Smith. 2008. "Cyberbullying: Another Main Type of Bullying?" *Scandinavian Journal of Psychology 49* (2): 147–54. https://doi.org/10.1111/j.1467-9450.2007.00611.x.

Smith, David, Michael McGowan, Christopher Knaus, and Nick Evershed. 2019. "Revealed: Ilhan Omar and Rashida Tlaib Targeted in Far-Right Fake News Operation." *The Guardian*, December 5, 2019, sec. Technology. https://www.theguardian.com/technology/2019/dec/05/ilhan-omar-rashida-tlaib-targeted-far-right-fake-news-operation-facebook.

Sobieraj, Sarah. 2019. "Disinformation, Democracy, and the Social Costs of Identity-Based Attacks Online." *MediaWell, Social Science Research Council*. October 22. https://mediawell.ssrc.org/expert-reflections/disinformation-democracy-and-the-social-costs-of-identity-based-attacks-online/.

Sobieraj, Sarah, Gina M. Masullo, Philip N. Cohen, Tarleton Gillespie, and Sarah J. Jackson. 2020. "Politicians, Social Media, and Digital Publics: Old Rights, New Terrain." Working Paper.

Sobieraj, Sarah, and Shaan Merchant. Forthcoming. "Gender and Race in the Digital Town Hall: Identity-Based Attacks against US Legislators on Twitter." In *Social Media and Social Order*.

Sojo, Victor E., Robert E. Wood, and Anna E. Genat. 2016. "Harmful Workplace Experiences and Women's Occupational Well-Being: A Meta-Analysis." *Psychology of Women Quarterly* 40 (1): 10–40. https://doi.org/10.1177/0361684315599346.

Somers, Margaret R. 1994. "The Narrative Constitution of Identity: A Relational and Network Approach." *Theory and Society* 23 (5): 605–49.

Squires, Catherine R. 2000. "Black Talk Radio: Defining Community Needs and Identity." *Harvard International Journal of Press/Politics* 5 (2): 73–95. https://doi.org/10.1177/1081180X00005002006.

Southern, Rosalynd, and Emily Harmer. 2019. "Twitter, Incivility and 'Everyday' Gendered Othering: An Analysis of Tweets Sent to UK Members of Parliament." *Social Science Computer Review* 35 (August): 84–102. https://doi.org/10.1177/0894439319865519.

Specia, Megan. 2019. "Threats and Abuse Prompt Female Lawmakers to Leave U.K. Parliament." *New York Times*, November 1, sec. World. https://www.nytimes.com/2019/11/01/world/europe/women-parliament-abuse.html.

Stanko, Elizabeth A. 1993. "The Case of Fearful Women." *Women & Criminal Justice* 4 (1): 117–35. https://doi.org/10.1300/J012v04n01_06.

Terpstra, David E., and Susan E. Cook. 1985. "Complainant Characteristics and Reported Behaviors and Consequences Associated with Formal Sexual Harassment Charges." *Personnel Psychology* 38 (3): 559–74. https://doi.org/10.1111/j.1744-6570.1985.tb00560.x.

Tucker, Joshua A., Andrew Guess, Pablo Barberá, Christian A. Vaccari, Alexandra Siegel, Sergey Sanovich, Denis Stukal, and Brendan Nyhan. 2018. "Social Media, Political Polarization, and Political Disinformation: A Review of the Scientific Literature." *William and Flora Hewlett Foundation*. https://poseidon01.ssrn.com/delivery.php?ID=299118127070014117107112065109121107103081020021005061018084073068096113022116013030107045042043006097108095117005117068027119042090023016077072107089112119070101020015077102116086014004031097082002098119097125006026110099086095070016023068112083100&EXT=pdf.

Tufekci, Zeynep, and Christopher Wilson. 2012. "Social Media and the Decision to Participate in Political Protest: Observations from Tahrir Square." *Journal of Communication* 62 (2): 363–79. https://doi.org/10.1111/j.1460-2466.2012.01629.x.

Turkle, Sherry. 1984. *The Second Self: Computers and the Human Spirit*. New York: Simon & Schuster.

"The Twitter Rules." n.d. Accessed January 26, 2020. https://help.twitter.com/en/rules-and-policies/twitter-rules.

Tworek, Heidi. 2019. "Social Media Councils." Models for Platform Governance. Centre for International Governance Innovation. https://www.cigionline.org/articles/social-media-councils.

Vaidhyanathan, Siva. 2018. *Antisocial Media: How Facebook Disconnects Us and Undermines Democracy*. New York: Oxford University Press.

Valentine, Gill. 1989. "The Geography of Women's Fear." *Area 21* (4): 385–90.

Veletsianos, George, Shandell Houlden, Jaigris Hodson, and Chandell Gosse. 2018. "Women Scholars' Experiences with Online Harassment and Abuse: Self-Protection, Resistance, Acceptance, and Self-Blame." *New Media & Society 20* (12): 4689–708. https://doi.org/10.1177/1461444818781324.

Wajcman, Judy. 2010. "Feminist Theories of Technology." *Cambridge Journal of Economics 34* (1): 143–52. https://doi.org/10.1093/cje/ben057.

Wajcman, Judy. 2004. *TechnoFeminism*. Malden, MA: Polity.

Wardle, Claire, and Hossein Derakhshan. 2017. "Information Disorder: Toward an Interdisciplinary Framework for Research and Policy Making." Council of Europe, October 31.

Welsh, Sandy. 1999. "Gender and Sexual Harassment." *Annual Review of Sociology 25* (1): 169–90. https://doi.org/10.1146/annurev.soc.25.1.169.

Wesely, Jennifer K., and Emily Gaarder. 2004. "The Gendered 'Nature' of the Urban Outdoors: Women Negotiating Fear of Violence." *Gender & Society 18* (5): 645–63. https://doi.org/10.1177/0891243204268127.

Williams, Christine L., Patti A. Giuffre, and Kirsten Dellinger. 1999. "Sexuality in the Workplace: Organizational Control, Sexual Harassment, and the Pursuit of Pleasure." *Annual Review of Sociology 25* (1): 73–93. https://doi.org/10.1146/annurev.soc.25.1.73.

Wong, Queenie. 2019. "Murders and Suicides: Here's Who Keeps Them Off Your Facebook Feed." *CNET*, March 1, 2019. https://www.cnet.com/news/facebook-content-moderation-is-an-ugly-business-heres-who-does-it/.

Young, Iris Marion. 2002. *Inclusion and Democracy*. Oxford: Oxford University Press.

Zippel, Kathrin S. 2006. *The Politics of Sexual Harassment: A Comparative Study of the United States, the European Union, and Germany*. Cambridge: Cambridge University Press.

Index

For the benefit of digital users, indexed terms that span two pages (e.g., 52–53) may, on occasion, appear on only one of those pages.